LIVING THE
HONEYMOON
Life

LIVING THE
HONEYMOON
Life

A Field Guide to the Seasons
of a Christ-Centered Marriage

TERRI KRUPP

Living the Honeymoon Life: *A Field Guide to the Seasons of a Christ-Centered Marriage*

Copyright ©2025 by Terri Krupp

https://LivingtheHoneymoonLife.com

Published by Life of Diamond

First edition

ISBN: 979-8-9924790-3-4 (Paperback)

ISBN: 979-8-9924790-4-1 (Hardcover)

ISBN: 979-8-9924790-5-8 (eBook)

Library of Congress Control Number: 2025910877

Book Coach: Bonnie Daneker, The Author's Greenhouse

Editing: David Aretha, www.DavidAretha.com

Illustrator: Jill Krupp

Cover Design and Interior Formatting: Becky's Graphic Design,® LLC
www.BeckysGraphicDesign.com

Printed in the United States of America

Publisher's Cataloging-in-Publication Data

Names: Krupp, Terri, author.

Title: Living the honeymoon life : a field guide to the seasons of a Christ-centered marriage / Terri Krupp.

Description: Heath, TX: Life of Diamond, 2025.

Identifiers: LCCN: 2025910877 | ISBN: 979-8-9924790-4-1 (hardcover) | 979-8-9924790-3-4 (paperback) | 979-8-9924790-5-8 (ebook)

Subjects: LCSH Marriage--Religious aspects--Christianity. | Marriage. | Christian life. | Happiness. | BISAC RELIGION / Christian Living / Love & Marriage | FAMILY & RELATIONSHIPS / Marriage & Long-Term Relationships

Classification: LCC BV4596 .K78 2025 | DDC 248.844--dc23

This book is, of course, first and foremost dedicated to Jesus, our Lord and Savior. However, enduring the writing process — when your skills are aligned in math and science — requires a purpose for the message to be shared. My purpose in starting this book is you - every Christian married couple who is committed to being salt and light in this world, to the best of their ability by the power of the Holy Spirit.

Curtis is my rock on this earth. He fiercely protects and loves me. He is the reason I can be so brave. I am richly blessed to have such a great example of Christ's love in my husband. So, to him I dedicate FINISHING the book.

Contents

Foreword   ix

  How to Use This Book   xi

  Honeymoon Life   1

Spring   9

  The Season   11

  Who Am I in Christ?   19

  Ingredients—Alignment and Peace   31

  Recipe for a Strong Marriage   37

  Fresh Starts and Do-Overs   45

  Krupp Marriage Experience   47

Summer   55

  The Season   57

  Who Am I in Christ?   67

  Ingredients—Yoked in Marriage, Work, and Mission   77

  Recipe for a Strong Marriage   85

  Fresh Starts and Do-Overs   95

  Krupp Marriage Experience   99

Autumn   109

  The Season   111

  Who Am I in Christ?   121

  Ingredients—Say You Are My Sister   129

  Reflections for a Strong Marriage   133

  Fresh Starts and Do-Overs   147

  Krupp Marriage Experience   153

Winter   159

   The Season   161

   Who Am I in Christ?   171

   Ingredients—Falling from Grace   177

   Recipe for a Strong Marriage   185

   Fresh Starts and Do-Overs   199

   Krupp Marriage Experience   205

Acknowledgments   211

Notes   213

Resources   215

   About the Author   217

   About the Illustrator   219

FOREWORD

To put the world in order, we must first put the nation
in order; to put the nation in order, we must first put
the family in order; to put the family in order, we must
first cultivate our personal life; and to cultivate our
personal life, we must first set our hearts right.

—CONFUCIUS

EVEN AN OSTRICH with its head in the ground could see that the
traditional marriage and family is becoming an endangered species.
Fewer people are getting married, and a higher percentage of married
people are getting divorced—a double whammy. Over one-fifth of
women NEVER marry. America is in a crisis.

In 1950, approximately 65 percent of women were married; now,
less than half are married. American couples are marrying later and
divorcing earlier. And having fewer children. Worldwide, this is a
challenge as well. Some ethnic groups will become minorities in their
own country within a generation or two—Japan, Russia, Greece, Italy,
Spain, and most European countries.

What is the number one cause of divorce? Seventy-five percent of
respondents in a long-term study cited the lack of commitment as the
leading cause of divorce. This can manifest as emotional withdrawal
and difficulty resolving conflicts constructively.

Terri and Curtis Krupp have found truths that have kept their
romance alive and actually deepened their commitment to traditional
marriage—making it virtually divorce-proof.

I have personally witnessed their life of love, faith, and devotion
to God and each other. For six years, they were part of a great move

of God in miracles and healing that was happening in the church I pastored.

They now offer to share what made the difference in their marriage in this book. All marriages seem to begin with perfect love and optimism, but few couples are able to sustain their passion. Men are not loving their wives the way the wives WANT to be loved, but the way they themselves want to be loved. And vice versa. Couples complain that they do not understand each other. Many just need a little help. Reading this and doing some of the exercises can put you in the mindset to increase that love, faith, and devotion to God and to your spouse.

—Pastor Robb Finberg, *Grace Church Maui*

How to Use
This Book

WE BELIEVE THAT "Practice Makes Permanent" and "How You Train is How You Fight." To that end, we have included ideas to integrate these suggestions into your regular routines:

- Pray together and separately for the Holy Spirit to guide you in this journey

- Set a time to read together and do activities. (This should become your first calendar habit if you do not already practice it.)

- Begin in the season that is most relevant to your current marriage/family

  - **Winter**: going through prolonged or serious issue
  - **Spring**: facing major changes such as moving, new baby, new job, going back to college
  - **Summer**: busy child-rearing or professional season
  - **Autumn**: slowing down, approaching empty-nesting or career retirement

- Use activities as opportunities to grow your relationship

- Adjust suggestions to fit you and your spouse's love languages (*See Resources section to learn more about Gary Chapman's work: he literally wrote the book on it.*)

- Test drive any changes you make to your current habits. Some you will not find useful or reasonable. Some you will make new habits to become permanent.

- Laugh! Probably the best advice we can give. Just enjoy the journey!

Watch for These Icons:

EACH ACTIVITY IS designed to keep the journey interesting and on track.

 FUN AND GAMES will ask you to stop and interact or set a time later to follow the prompt.

 **TRUE NORTH** will ask you to quiet yourselves and let the message settle in. May have a time suggestion.

 **WORK IT OUT Together** is the practical application. It requires individual and mutual input, honesty and vulnerability. This is where the rubber meets the road, these activities give you insights and plans to institute into your marriage. Do not rush these activities. We have found if we take time to contemplate the questions, we discover way more about each other than we anticipated.

 **SALT AND LIGHT** shows we are called to be salt and light to this world. These fun little observations or insights help to highlight how and when we have seen it manifested.

 **CURTIS' INPUT** WILL balance the work. He is generally a very quiet and reserved personality, but he is very wise and insightful, and his view should not be missed. (Curtis is a devout Weber Smoker man, do not offer him a gas grill, you have been warned.)

FAITH JOURNEY ADDS additional study, consideration and insight. Taking what you are learning to a deeper level together builds the foundational habit of meeting God in the garden in the cool of the day, our original intended blessing. If it is helpful at the moment, it is there for use; if it is a distraction from your progress at the moment, come back to it later.

Living the Honeymoon Life gives specific examples of how Curtis and I have made these habits work.

Honeymoon Life

On a Mission from God!

IN THE 1980 comedy/adventure hit *The Blues Brothers*, Elwood and Jake Blues set out on a quest to raise $5,000 to save the Catholic Home where they were raised. As they put it, "We are on a mission from God." While the example is slightly ridiculous, we all are on a mission from God, even in our marriages.

Our calling for Honeymoon Life came subtly. After decades of marriage, raising children, moving, layoffs, and owning a franchise, we have remained best friends and passionately affectionate to one another. Over the decades, Curtis and I have received different assignments and callings from God: youth leader, sound booth technician, hula dancer, Sunday School teacher, group leader, women's group leader, baseball team coach, and more. . . but being called to share about God's heart for marriage and the original design set forth in the Garden of Eden has been a true surprise to us.

Many in our circle find it unusual and call our relationship an anomaly. Ours should not be the outlier, but the norm. In the beginning, God established man and wife to be the closest representation of His love for this world, an image of what was to come through Jesus. Covenant marriage, two becoming one flesh, is a reflection of the restoration Jesus gives through salvation.

God accomplished His ultimate plan to restore His relationship with mankind through the blood and sacrifice of His Son. Jesus, the bridegroom, is the head of the Church. Husbands, God expects Christian married men to reflect Christ's servant leadership to your wife. Wives, you are as the Church, the Bride of Christ, are intended to be the perfect helper, unblemished, and fit for Kingdom work. Christ and the Church are the ultimate marriage; you and your spouse in Holy Covenant reflect how God brought His plan to pass.

A friend captured this photo of Curtis and Terri in Verona, Italy in 1988.

Our Genesis—I Know You!

The curious story of how Curtis and I met began with me being on temporary duty with the United States Air Force in Turkey, coming back through Germany. I was visiting friends in Ramstein during a four-day layover. They had a friend who hung out with us as well— Curtis was the mutual friend.

When we first met, I recognized how handsome he was, but ours was just friendship. We shared interests in music and games, and we played chess several times. We had some conversations about our careers in the Air Force. He asked me where I was going to "PCS" (permanent change of station) and I said, "Aviano, Italy." He said,

"Really, that's where I'm going," but I took it as a pick-up line, not necessarily the truth.

Well, a few months later, I did PCS to Aviano, Italy. Before I could leave the base, I needed to complete my cultural training. It ended on a Friday, so my friends decided it was a good idea to thrust me heavily into Italian culture by taking me to Carnevale. Carnevale is Mardi Gras in Venice, one of the biggest celebrations on the Italian calendar.

We arrived in Venice after a crowded train ride, which had provided much more elbow room and breathing space than the crowd in Venice. It was packed canal to canal. You could barely stream your way two-deep through the streets.

As the day turned to late afternoon and evening, I was starting to gain some confidence moving through the people. A man approached me and said, "I know you." This young American had makeup smeared across his face and had clearly drunk too much canal water. I maneuvered my way around him, but he followed me and persisted. "No really. I know that girl, Terri!" he said to his friends. Well, that stopped me in my tracks.

Out of probably one million people crowded into a few square miles, someone had found their way to me. It was Curtis.

CURTIS' INPUT

Greatest Pick-up Line Ever

A group of us young American men headed to Carnevale late morning. We put some makeup on our faces for the occasion, grabbed a boda bag of wine, and brought our great expectations. There were supposed to be memorable festivities and, of course, beautiful Italian girls just dying to meet us.

The first part was correct. Knowing very little Italian and enjoying too much "canal water," as Terri coined it, made our success rate of impressing young ladies close to zero. But we would loudly say, "I know that dude!" as our introduction. I know, completely charming. We must have just watched Fast Times at Ridgemont High or something, because that is where the phrase originated. Sean Penn as

Jeff Spicoli, the constantly stoned high schooler, said that phrase a couple of times. Again, charming, right?

Anyhow, throughout the day of squeezing through the crowded Venice streets, we would occasionally get a chance to shout this phrase with minimal success using our broken Italian. The way I remember, my friend Fran and I were waiting for our friends, and he said, "Hey, it's your turn."

I was not enthusiastic as it was after 9 p.m. I looked over and exclaimed: "I know that dude!"

And he says, "Great!"

"No, I really know her!"

"Sure you do…"

My loud exclamation and pointing finger got the attention of my target. It was Terri!

THROUGH EVENTS LIKE Carnevale, Curtis and I have seen the hand of a higher power working in our relationship. Over the decades, we have turned our focus off of each other and onto God. Keeping God as the head of our relationship has proven to be the most important step toward an intimate and passionate marriage union.

But Why a Book?

We are currently on a new health journey. Because of age and stress over the past few decades, our bodies are not where we want them to be physically. We have committed to make a change, working with health professionals and following their guidance to reclaim our optimum health. One of the key factors in making this change is the use of new recipes and new cookbooks to accomplish our healthy eating goals. My same old, memorized-by-heart recipes just cannot get us to where we want to be.

That is the purpose of this book. You may be longing for change in your marriage, but without new recipes of thinking and focus to guide your actions, the change will never come. In these how-to pages, we share the simple and fun methods that have brought our relationship with God, and with ourselves, to the highest level.

Speaking this message is meant to awaken the Church and dispel the lies that have been allowed to creep into our vocabularies, even among believers. While the lies often get the attention, let's focus on God's truths.

- **Truth**: One man and one woman becoming one flesh is God's covenant for marriage. The image of Christ and His Bride, the Church, are proof of His passion for His creation, specifically people.

- **Truth**: Claiming the empowering promise of "two or more gathered in My name, there I am with them." (Matthew 18:20) is a threat to Hell. By operating in unity and agreeing in Jesus' name, your marriage is a powerful force in the universe. That is why the enemy works so hard to undermine the purpose and foundation of marriage, especially among Christians.

- **Truth**: The honeymoon does last if it is rooted in our relationship with Christ.

To make the change and bring our relationships into alignment with God, we must practice new habits *Living the Honeymoon Life* is meant to be a springboard for this new way of life. To improve your health long-term, your food diet and activity schedule depend on small, consistent disciplines that you employ daily. Those are the building blocks of living the Honeymoon Life: consistent small habits and practices that build lasting, healthy, God-honoring marriages.

These inexpensive and simple-to-implement practices yield large dividends in your "love tank" deposits. These deposits can include loving, small gestures like holding hands while driving on errands or sitting on the couch up to large undertakings like creating a marriage mission. Throughout this book, we will explore a wide spectrum of ideas and fun tricks to invest in your marriage.

Why a Guide with Recipes? Why Birds?

Scientists have confirmed that the time spent around the table with family and friends is some of the most impactful relationship-building investments we can make. Most cultures' celebrations and holidays have particular foods associated with them. *Living the Honeymoon Life* capitalizes on the truth that food is an important part of the human experience.

Preparing for the wedding ceremony, the honeymoon, or even an important celebration requires an investment of time, resources, and emotional and mental input, so why would our marriages demand any less? Inside are simple recipes to follow to bring about the passionate, tender, and God-honoring marriage you desire, but it requires work. It is our prayer that you are able to glean from the suggestions and create your own Honeymoon Life reality.

The use of birds to begin each season is derived from birds having an important role in creation and the Bible. When Noah was looking for the waters to recede as God had promised, he sent out a dove. (Genesis 8:8) When Jesus was baptized, the Spirit descended on Him as a dove. (Matthew 3:16) We are reminded of God's promised care for us because He cares for the sparrow. (Matthew 6:26) When mighty plagues and massacres happened in the Old Testament, ravens were sent to clean the earth of the flesh. (Jeremiah 7:33) Birds are signs of promises kept, good coming to the land, strength, and ominous reminders that the curse is still very much in effect in this life. And they are beautiful reminders of the creative majesty of the Father.[1]

How to Get the Most Out of Your Time in This Book—Be a Good Date

When Curtis and I go out, we are almost always approached by strangers asking us how long we have been together. Our answer: "three. . . decades." (*That will only work for a few more years as we are entering our thirty-fifth year of marriage.*) They comment, "You two look like you are on a date." They are correct—we are always dating!

We hope that you and your spouse undertake this journey together as a good, long series of dates. On any journey, each step gets us that much closer to our goal, yet we will never be finished with this journey in this life. There is always room to grow closer together, stronger in faith, and bolder in action for the kingdom. Doing your marriage mission in unity with your spouse is the most rewarding undertaking you will find on this side of Heaven.

"...Being confident of this, that he who began a good work in you will carry it on to completion until the day of Christ Jesus." (Philippians 1:6) When we see Jesus, we will be perfected. Until then, we are still learning.

If you'd like to enjoy the Honeymoon Life, you can start today. It does not matter how and where your marriage began, how you met, or how big your issues have been. What matters is what you do from now on, moving forward and into the rest of your life. God is gracious and merciful. He uses ordinary people to accomplish His extraordinary purposes here on earth. He can—and does—use all of us to share His love to the world. We have made more than our share of mistakes, but God calls us into the mission field of life every day. It's our hope that these pages will help you reach your version of a powerful, loving, God-centered marriage.

Happy Honeymooning!

With Love,
Terri and Curtis Krupp

For a quick, personal message follow this link:
https://LivingtheHoneymoonLife.com

SPRING

EASTERN BLUEBIRDS

These little guys eat bugs and sit atop wires or posts to watch for crawling critters. They will sometimes pick up their prey or catch it mid-air to avoid landing on the ground. "As a courtship display, males may sing and flutter in front of the female with his wings and tail partly spread. While perched close together, pairs may preen each other's feathers; males may feed the female."[2] They are generally monogamous, proving even a bird brain knows one mate is enough. That's pretty romantic. The male sings to her and feeds her. They clean each other's feathers. Nothing says "I love you" like cleaning each other's feathers! When was the last time you and your spouse took time to go back to those precious courting practices that won you each other's hearts to begin with? If you can't name a date, it's been too long!

April Showers Bring May Flowers

If you are like me, you may have sung this ditty while splashing in a puddle. Notice what the little jingle tells us: It requires showers—rainy days—to bring about beauty, in the form of flowers. Those rainy days can make me tired, and I just want to snuggle in with a good book. The changing season can be exhausting because it requires something dying off in winter—new growth buds. The resulting flowers make those dreary days well worth enduring.

Likewise, your marriage will have rainy days and flowers. Times of change can bring on conflict and stress. Enduring the ending of known things in order to push for new beginnings. One way to ensure your marriage is up for the challenge is to reinforce your "teammates" mindset, where you and your spouse are acting together as a united force: You are connected and strengthened with the vision of what you both know your marriage is called to be and your planned goals of life together. Working together toward these shared goals, in covenant, requires unity. Let God's steadfastness be your anchor in times of change and take the Honeymoon Life challenge: While circumstances all around you swirl and shift, you are focused on the One who never fails!

Scripture to Memorize Together

"Therefore, if anyone is in Christ, he is a new creation; the old things passed away, behold new things have come.

2 CORINTHIANS 5:17

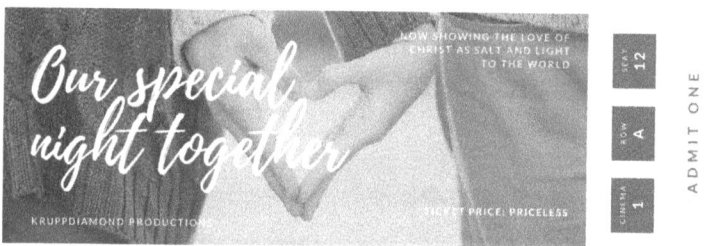

Consider making a physical date coupon or "event ticket." Hand-write and draw one, or, if you're feeling fancy, make one digitally and print it out.

The Season

CURTIS' INPUT

There Is No *I* in Marriage; Well, at Least in a Team Marriage

A marriage can be like an offense on a football team. Sometimes you are the star quarterback directing your team toward victory. Other times, you are a lineman who blocks so the quarterback can have time to throw a pass. Still other times, you are on the sidelines cheering on your team, waiting to be put in at the right time. All positions are necessary; some are just more high-profile.

IN THIS SEASON, it is imperative to have your eyes focused squarely on your mutual purpose and goals. During times of change, it can be easy to feel as if the earth is shifting beneath you. Jesus taught us that the wise person (wise marriage) built his house on the rock and not shifting sand. (*See Matthew 7:24-25.*) Building our foundation on the rock requires that each member of the team knows their value and worth in Christ. We must value each other and be determined to bring out the best in our spouses—their God-given gifts. This builds a unified team.

Physics Agrees

Newton's First Law of Motion states, "An object at rest will remain at rest, and an object in motion will continue moving with a constant velocity, unless acted upon by an external force."[3]

When you are united through Christ in Holy Matrimony, you are a force to be reckoned with in the Universe. Living in the power of new mercies every day is the force for change that will propel your marriage into the likeness of Christ's Bride.

Force—that's a pretty strong word. Spring is the season that brings changes as showers and warmer weather buds' life back into sight—which requires energy to accomplish. It's a time for renewal of what lay dormant during the inhospitable season of winter. Often, the process of change itself can usher in stress. It causes us to lose our current state of being, which we know, in exchange for the new stage that is unknown. Even the laws of physics reflect the reluctance to change.

"The only person that likes change is a wet baby."

SAYING ACCREDITED TO MARK TWAIN

What About Changes in Marriage?

Marriages, even long-lasting romances, go through seasons. For example, the presence of children brings change. In the beginning you are living life together as a couple, then your house is full of children, and later the children move on. Each stage is a change that must be adapted to.

It is natural and healthy to experience change; the key is how we manage these events. In the previous example, think about your response when the children leave or have left. What will be the focus of your attention when the nest is empty? If you have a household built around the children and their activities, you may be left feeling like the house and the relationship are truly empty.

The dynamic of two is a powerful force in the universe: Where two or more are gathered in my name, He (God) is there. (*See Matthew 18:20.*) We cannot accomplish this on our own. We need God's influence to unite us together as one and lead us in His path of growing us. A marriage that reflects God's design has Him as the focal point of all that the couple does. Like winter giving way to spring, dark and difficult seasons can sprout beautiful new growth when given the proper attention and care.

Answering the Call

Sometimes, answering the call means EVERYTHING changes. Here's an example. It was a beautiful spring day in our small, rural Iowa town. Curtis was outside attending to some yard work, with all four of our children at hand to help or climb trees, whichever the moment commanded. I had a rare late morning of undisturbed housework, and I was diligently cycling through as much as I could multitask while the getting was good. Of course, I had my worship music cranked way up for encouragement.

The landline rang and I hurried to answer it. In those days we had one cell phone that we used for only necessary calls on the go. If a neighbor or family member was trying to reach us, they would call the home phone first; if we did not answer, they would try the cell. Wanting to avoid using precious minutes, I tried to catch the caller before three or four rings, because then the answering machine would intervene.

I answered in my customary friendly greeting, expecting to hear a familiar voice or a telemarketer. The caller on the other end surprised me and said, "Hello, this is Dan Kokubun, calling from Honolulu, Hawaii. I am trying to reach Curtis Krupp."

Baffled, I inquired, "May I ask what this is regarding?"

"Yes, I am with STI, and we are reaching out about an open position we have here in Honolulu."

More suspicious than stunned, I played along and asked "Mr. Kokubun" to hold while I retrieved Curtis. I took the hand-held phone receiver out to him. Once outside, I quickly summarized what the caller had said, and we looked at each other in wonder. Receiving a call from someone named "Kokubun" immediately set off alarm bells. Additionally, a top suspect for a prank call would have been one of Curtis' best friends from the Air Force whose initials are S.T., so STI, Honolulu? *Come on, Shawn,* I thought. *You can do better than that.*

Curtis went in to take the call and I stayed outside watching our children and some neighborhood kids playing without a care in the world. This was a wonderful place to raise children, and with the youngest of four just about to turn two, it was hard to imagine a better life for them. Our beautiful property consisted of an overly large, extremely productive garden in which I spent the bulk of the growing season. It had a bountiful pear tree, an apple tree, and four plum trees. All of the produce was processed and canned so that nothing went to waste. Our son consumed the lion's share of the pears, eating them at any stage of ripeness.

CURTIS' INPUT

Dan Who?

"Dan who?" I asked. I had that face that looked confused and disbelieving.

"Dan Cocoa Buns or something," Terri said, covering the receiver. "He is from a company in Hawaii. It's about a job." Her facial expression gave me no clue on who was on the line.

So, I accepted the phone from my lovely wife and started talking. The voice seemed vaguely familiar. He asked some basic questions that anyone in an interview would know to ask. He did have all my personal information down pat. He asked if Hawaii and the job interested me. He really started sounding like my best friend from the Air Force, Shawn. The more he spoke, the more I was convinced that it was him. Terri looked at me, and I mouthed, "I think it is Shawn." I was smiling now. I thought I would go along with it for a minute. Then, he made me certain he was NOT Shawn. He said he had "found my resume on the SPIE job board. . ." Yeah, you don't know what that is either. It is a site that is very specific to optics jobs. Shawn wouldn't know that. My smile changed, and I left Terri with the kids. This was a real opportunity; one I hadn't applied for!

The interview went well, so we scheduled a group interview for the following week, which went well also. Then silence. . . For nearly two weeks! I called Dan Kokubun. He wasn't worried. HR would call me. He would reach out to them. I believe by the time it was all said and done; it took over a month for HR to talk to me so I could accept the position. Dan informed me that people in Hawaii didn't rush to get things done. It's called "Island Time."

FULL DISCLOSURE, WE had recently made the decision to put Curtis' resume back out into the pool of candidates, even if it required us to move. He was at a crossroads with needing to get back into his exact specialty or never having hope of further pursuing his career as a laser-electro optics technician again. It had been less than a month prior to this call when I had prayed out loud, in Curtis' hearing, "Lord, if we must move from this wonderful home, I want it to be to Hawaii!" I want you to understand, Curtis had never applied for this position, or any position with STI. This was completely a "God love note!"

After the offer came, the process moved very quickly. Within weeks, Curtis had accepted the offer, and we were moving to Honolulu, Hawaii. God has a beautiful sense of humor. So many questions to be answered and an overwhelming number of plans needed to be arranged before I could leave for the Island with our four children. The decision was made for Curtis to leave and for us to follow once he could secure us a place to live.

Out of faith, before the call had even come through, I had begun my part of the burden of preparation by downsizing and organizing our six-person, three-and-a-half-story Victorian home. We had moved a few times before, since leaving the Air Force, but those moves had included only Curtis and me, and then the last move from Colorado to Iowa with only our oldest. This move, if it happened, was going to require a lot more lead time. And a bit of downsizing of material possessions, which is generally in order every few years anyway, especially in a family this size.

In our little Iowa paradise, we had built a huge community within our neighborhood and church. All of my family lived within an hour's drive, and the holidays were packed with our loved ones. I was nervous, to put it mildly, and as I often do when I am unsure of my ability to follow God's plan, I started making demands in my prayers. "Fine, Lord, I will go, but I am NOT going to attend a big church!" In my heart I heard God laugh.

In our current little church, we were youth leaders, Sunday school teachers, ushers. We had an amazing small group that had seen us through some very difficult seasons. We loved the way our pastor preached unapologetically the Word of God. That is number one for us in our church. Leaving this support and comfort was not what we had wanted for our family, but God had made it very clear: He wanted us on the Islands.

Curtis secured a minivan and a condo that would be available a week after the kids, and I arrived. For the interim, STI had agreed to put us up in a house on the Windward side of the island, right off the beach. That first week on Oahu was like a dream. My uncle lives in the little beach town of Kailua, just up from where our rental was, and we got to know him and his family very well. Kailua Beach consistently rates among the top beaches in the world. (We were just up the coast from where *Magnum, P.I.*, the television series, was filmed.) Curtis worked during the day, and the kids and I would get up, pack a cooler, and head to the beach on foot. We would come back for a cool-down just before Curtis got home, and then the family would head back to the beach for the evening swim. On weekends we would explore the island, finding other beaches, local hotspots, and "ono kine grinds." (That is the locals' way of saying "good food.") That season remains one of the most precious times in our family's history.

As with every move, we had found a church home. Well, this time God had not honored my whining. We landed at New Hope Fellowship,

Oahu, the fastest-growing church in the nation at that time. The kids and I got involved in the Kempo Karate ministry as well as the youth programs. There was so much opportunity to serve and get plugged in that we quickly made friends. Curtis' work became more demanding, and we decided he would get his next degree. He studied while the kids and I slept in on weekends. The kids' school and extracurricular activities quickly picked up, and we were back to full swing.

We embraced change. We tuned our hearts together to learn and experience a whole new world that we had never known. Curtis and I had moved many times, but our children were getting a total change of everything they had known all at once. As a family we stuck together, learned, and loved the culture as we made Hawaii our home for the next eight years.

Who Am I in Christ?

To Whom Do I Belong?

TO HAVE HEALTHY, meaningful relationships, we must be firmly grounded in who we are created to be and reflect back who carefully attended to us as we were formed. The fact is that you are fearfully and wonderfully made!

> For you formed my inward parts; you wove me in my mother's womb. I will give thanks to you, for I am fearfully and wonderfully made; Wonderful are your works, and my soul knows it very well.
>
> **PSALM 139:13-14**

See if you can imagine what it was like when you were in your mother's womb. You are just a couple of cells, reproducing as instructed by each DNA strand. The process is complicated and involved. Each replication is a chemical process to marvel. Just the number of exact perfect events that need to occur for a human being to be completed is staggering! We are not an accident of chemistry. Our DNA is fantastic, but it's fantastic because God is fantastic. There are no mistakes in DNA. There are flaws, but they reflect the fallen world we live in. So whatever strengths and weaknesses you have been made with, they were allowed in you to share with this world.

Try to meditate on the fact that you once were a helpless, innocent baby. If you're a parent yourself or have even witnessed a dog having puppies or a cat having kittens, you can appreciate what an amazing and miraculous event birth is. (Jesus also experienced this vulnerable human condition.) An intimate and powerful reality occurs when we embrace what it means to be formed in the womb.

We must make this psalm our posture—that we are miraculously designed. With that in mind, it will be impossible to miss what God has planned for us in this life. God designed us to be full of passion, creative, and intimate, living abundant lives. Jesus' life is proof of that.

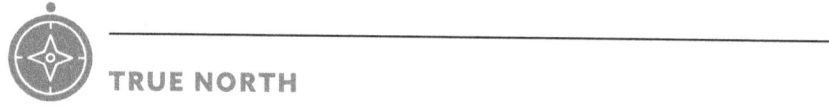

TRUE NORTH

30 Seconds on the Clock

Take a moment right now. Pause. Take time to thank God, personalizing the paraphrased scripture below.

"I, ___(name)_____, am fearfully and wonderfully made. You watched over every aspect of my development and growth. You intentionally put me in this place at this time with talents and gifts that are uniquely mine! Thank you, Father. Amen!"

Foundation of Being Perfectly and Wonderfully Made in Our Roles as Husband and Wife by God's Order

How does this relate to marriage? We must learn to appreciate our spouses for their God-given gifts. Once we apply this precious truth about our formations to ourselves and our spouses, we have a foundation to build upon. We need the precious gifts of both husband and wife.

God's design for marriage is revealed from the beginning of the Bible. (*See Genesis 1:27*) God speaks, and man is created in His image, male and female. God made us to reflect his full nature. Adam was not a complete image without the female piece in place (something was missing).

Now God is not a woman, and He's not just a man. The best way we can fully understand God is to look at both male and female strengths. He reveals that the female characteristics also reflect his omnipotent nature. To get the best picture of the lovingkindness of our Creator, we look to both male and female traits in one flesh. We are a reflection of who He is and what His heart is toward this world.

In creation, the male was first. God "formed" Adam out of the dirt. (*See Genesis 2:7*) He is gritty and happy to muscle through to get the job done. (I've used this with Curtis a few times, that "Adam was made out of dirt." Let's just be honest that there was a certain rawness to Adam; you know, elemental. Men, we love you for that!)

But God exclaims, "It's not good for the man to be alone." (Genesis 2:18b) This is the only thing in all of creation that was declared "not good." There was an incompleteness to Adam being alone. He was insufficient by himself to reflect and accomplish all of God's purpose. He needed a partner to "subdue and conquer the earth," not to mention to "be fruitful and multiply." (Genesis 1:28)

After this declaration God introduces Eve, the suitable helper. Verse 18 states, "It is not good for the man to be alone; I will make a helper suitable for him." She was to complete him, complement and add to his identity. After God looked on the loneliness of man, He "fashioned" woman out of Adam's rib. (*See Genesis 2:22*) "The man said, 'This is now bone of my bones, and flesh of my flesh; she shall be called Woman, because she was taken out of man'." (Genesis 2:23)

As women, we are designed to be beautiful artwork. (Sisters, we put the WO in woman!)

Gentlemen, when you look and see that fashioned woman of yours, remember, it isn't easy or cheap to keep that up. It may cost you a body part.

 FAITH JOURNEY

The Mystery is Great

Read Genesis 1:26-31: God created Male and Female to be His hands and feet in ruling over the rest of creation.

Genesis 2:18-24: Creation before Eve left a gap that God needed to expand His presence into. Man being alone without his counterpart does not allow for the union of two becoming one flesh.

Man was never designed to be without a helper. Eve was the suitable fulfillment of that need, that lack. God completed creation by creating two creatures that fuse together to become one. It is a great mystery.

The Only Marriage Advice Worth Passing Along

When I was a teenager, I spent many of my weekends, when I was not busy with school activities, traveling on lay witness mission (LWM) trips. These trips were aimed at helping little churches breathe life into their congregations. It would often bring a fire of the Holy Spirit into their youth program and their church as a whole.

One particular LWM group I participated in was led by an old farmer and his old wife. They had been married longer than I knew people could live. He had lost one arm at the elbow in a combine accident, and his wife was a meek and quiet farmer's wife.

When I was about fifteen years old, this barn preacher gave a teaching to our youth group. He taught us what it meant to truly be yoked as Christ designed it. He told us, "Marriage is not 50/50. It's 100 percent/100 percent." That was mind-blowing. I had never heard anyone teach about marriage like that. He was saying that marriage is not a give-and-take; it's give-and-give. Jesus modeled that kind of sold-out, servant leadership to His followers and to us His bride, the Church. It is the true design God gave us to become one flesh.

The preacher also challenged us to start praying for our spouse—not praying for who we would get as a spouse, and not a romantic notion of happily ever after, but that our intended spouse would be protected and make wise decisions along the way. Although naïve, at the age of fifteen, I began praying for my future spouse. Both of us, it turned out, made many mistakes and poor dating choices along the way, but God is faithful and brought us through so we could eventually meet. Curtis and I both needed the prayer of others to get us to the place where God could bring us together.

We continue to make praying for each other a priority. We have adopted a 100 percent/100 percent commitment to our marriage. We still have difficult days, arguments, and misunderstandings. There is no perfect relationship except between Jesus and His Bride, the Church. Perfection is not the goal; persistence is!

I Like You

The most difficult part of marriage can be allowing for failure. I mean, we can still love someone without liking them sometimes. When I made the grievous error of hitting two of our cars together, Curtis did not yell or blame or shame me. He quietly worked two weekends in the garage to fix things and still managed to LIKE me.

CURTIS' INPUT

My Side of the Story

When your wife calls and says she has gotten into a little fender bender, you figure there are no injuries and minimal damage. This was mostly true when Terri called. Unfortunately, she let me know that the fender-bender she got into was with our two cars! Just there in the driveway. I was grateful she was uninjured, but seriously?

Repairing the two cars was a process that took a couple of weekends with little cost, but much labor. On the second weekend, I remember I was struggling a little with the repair, and my lovely bride comes out to ask how things are going. Well, I just looked at her and was a bit speechless. Then, a phrase came out that we still say. I unemotionally said, "I like you."

She kind of stood there for a few seconds and then went into the house.

TO TRULY EMBRACE God's design for our marriages, we each must fulfill our God-designated roles:

Wife, you are a jewel, one that he can't take his eye off of. You are fearfully and wonderfully made, fashioned to be beautiful and desirable to your husband. Your role is to uplift him and bring his Godly character to the surface for the usefulness of the Kingdom. Live in this confidence and walk in this assuredness—blessed assuredness—that you are God's child first but also fall under your husband's protection.

Husband, you are the rock and the safe place your wife longs to be. You are fearfully and wonderfully made. When you truly live out your calling as spiritual leader of the family, provider, protector, and worshiper, you bring such comfort and peace to your wife. She knows she is safe in your arms. "Husbands, love your wives, just as Christ also loved the church and gave Himself up for her." (Ephesians 5: 25)

Because God chose to create us in His image, He needed to include both the male and female to fully reflect His capacity for love and creativity and unity. Man was better fit for his calling after Eve was created. Within that blueprint, the man could count on the woman to support and speak life into what God had called him to be. The woman can rest assured that her husband was her protection and provider.

A husband answers to God, then he leads his wife in the likeness of Christ. The wife upholds the order and peace of God in service to Christ and her husband. Don't let the current culture confuse you; there is a good purpose to God's alignment. The word *submission* is not our enemy. If we start this relationship with that in place, we can each live out our full calling in our day-to-day lives. We can reflect God's original design for our union.

It is so easy to get stuck in a "him vs. her" or "her vs. him" mindset. I was reading *Marketplace Marriage and Revival* by Jack Serra. He tells a story about praying to God to change his wife. Jack writes, "I was asking the Lord to make my wife more tactful, loving, and kind. God said, "How dare you ask me to change what I have created perfectly for my purposes?"[4]

Funny. I, too, encountered the same response when I prayed for God to change my husband: "God, you see this man and how he needs to change!" God replied. "This is MY son, and I love him just as he is!"

With this perspective we can appreciate our spouses and be grateful to the Lord for the gift of our spouses in our lives, just as they are created. Let's set our hearts in the right position by praying this prayer over our spouse as often as necessary.

Spouses' Serenity Prayer

God, grant me the peace to understand that my spouse was created exactly as you desired, for exactly the purposes you have, with all of the ability you implanted to become the best that they can be. While neither of us is perfect, you have bound us together in your perfect union, to experience the fullness of your love and your life, and reflect YOUR perfection in this marriage, to carry your light in this dark world. Our marriage, anointed in your grace and full of your purpose, is the best reflection of Christ and the Church we can offer as a testimony.

BY TERRI KRUPP
(ADAPTED FROM REINHOLD NIEBUHR'S
"AA SERENITY PRAYER.")

Being United in One Flesh—Agreeing with God's Plan

We are united in a covenant with God as individuals, then as husband and wife. The husband is aligned under and united in a covenant with God; He is the director. God is the first order, the first rung on the organizational chart, with the husband directly under God. The wife is uniquely positioned under her husband, not as a sub-servant or less significant, but for an added layer of protection to her. Then, they are united as one flesh living in their marriage bond.

Fully bringing God's image into the world requires the two becoming one flesh. Think about your body. If you want your hand to lift a bag of groceries, you must get your brain, arm, and back involved. Your hand does not act alone; it is following the guidance and prompting of the nervous and muscular systems. Becoming one flesh requires some tuning of our brain to God for the information we need. Utilizing our muscular system, our marriages, we bring purpose into fullness.

The husband-and-wife cling to each other as one flesh and work together as one system. This truth is so crucial that Jesus quotes the scripture of Genesis when the Pharisees attempted to stump him about divorce. (*See Mark 10:7-9*) How can we truly become one flesh? Think of these two Scripture passages:

- "The things that are impossible with people are possible with God." (Luke 18:27)
- "Draw near to God and He will draw near to you. Cleanse your hands, you sinners and purify your hearts, you double-minded." (James 4: 8)

Speaking, thinking, and acting as the rest of the world does keeps us from living Christ-like. The same is true in marriage. We must honor God's way of the man being the head of the household as Christ is of the Church. A body cannot function in doublemindedness. Two heads in a marriage are NOT better than one. The senior pastor of Lakepointe Church, Josh Howerton, put it this way: "A body without a head is a corpse. A body with two heads is a freak."

 **WORK IT OUT TOGETHER**

Considerations

	HIS	HERS	OURS
WE ARE ONE FLESH: HOW WILL I LIVE DIFFERENTLY?			
I FEEL MOST UNIFIED WITH YOU WHEN… (Let that go wherever it leads)			
I AM EXCITED TO _____ WITH YOU.			
ON A SCALE OF 1-10 (LOW TO HIGH) HOW RICH AND PASSIONATE IS OUR MARRIAGE?			

Reflections of the Marriage Between the Lamb and His Bride, the Church

We, as married Christian couples, have the potential to be firsthand evidence of Christ's love for His Bride, the Church. But it can only come after we do the deep work of living in and accepting our personal identity in Christ.

I struggled with this reality most of my life. I am not a "girly girl." My only aspiration as I grew up was to be an astronaut. I was a tomboy, and I never really thought of myself as beautiful, especially in the womanly sense, and certainly not a fashionista.

I remember a day after we had moved to Oahu, when I saw hula dancing in person for the first time. I thought to myself, *those are the most beautiful women on earth.* They came in all shapes and sizes, and I appreciated that because they *all* looked elegant.

When we moved to Maui, I was invited into a Hula Ministry at church. I am not the most graceful, and it fell outside of my gifts. I love dancing—the kind where I get out on the floor and make a fool of myself and embarrass my children—but I never thought of myself as a graceful dancer. After months and months of practice, I was worshiping in church with the ministry. I remember dancing, and for the first time in my life, I could feel the adoration, the preciousness that God found in me. As I hula danced, I understood as a woman that I was beautiful. A beauty that is not just about a physical aura, but a resplendent purpose for me exactly as I am. This truth is deep down buried in who you are. You might be a little bit clumsy. Your hands might not have elegance. Your feet might not move lightly, and your sway might not be perfect and timed in unison with everyone else's. But, if you will worship Holy (and wholly) and raw before the God who created you, I promise you that you will understand that He finds you beautiful and He wants nothing more than for you to live that life of understanding. This new identity may take some getting used to, but it is part of living our marriage as a reflection of the marriage between Christ and His Bride, the Church.

CURTIS' INPUT

Hula as Worship

Terri is right on here—Hula is resplendent. When Terri started practicing Hula at Grace Church Maui, I was excited in a selfish way. I couldn't wait until she would do a personal Hula for me. Then when she and the other dancers worshiped in Church for God, I knew it would never happen. This dance was not just some way to romance your spouse; it was truly spiritual worship. Hula speaks to God.

Men, This Message Is For You As Well

YOU ARE HIS dear and precious son. He could not be more pleased with you! No matter where you've gone and what you've done, no matter how you've compromised, there is nothing more intimate than you turning to Him and saying, "Father, I want to be home with You."

In the Spring, the season of change, it is important to stay firmly rooted in your NEW identity in Christ. No matter what your age, you can always embrace the fresh newness of being in Christ.

TRUE NORTH

Making It Personal

Let's get back to the mindset of a Honeymoon Life that honors and walks daily with God with another activity. It's time to personalize and memorize this next verse from scripture.

The original: "Therefore, if anyone is in Christ, this person is a new creation; the old things passed away, behold new things have come." (Memory Verse: 2 Corinthians 5:17)

Personalized: Therefore, if _____(name) is in Christ, he/she is a new creation; the old things _____ (past hurts or disappointments) have passed away, behold new things _____ (how I am living differently) have come.

To put this all together: The moment we join in the covenant of marriage, we become one new flesh joined together. Because Christ died to give us forgiveness and reconciliation with God the Father, we cannot be held captive by our past persona; we must move toward our new identity, united in Christ. Our marriage falls under this same promise. In committing our marriage fully and completely to Jesus, in the power of the Holy Spirit, we can become a bold, shining example of God's Love in this world.

SPRING

Ingredients— Alignment and Peace

Biblical Couple: Isaac and Rebekah

THEY WERE LITERALLY a match made in heaven. Abraham sent his servant to retrieve a wife for Isaac, his promised son. The servant prayed for the success of the mission because he loved his master. The servant's prayer was answered in the exact way that he had requested. After returning with the "Prayer Order Bride," Isaac and Rebekah immediately fell in love. What a love story, and what an answer to prayer!

Unlike a Hallmark movie, that is not where the story ends. As in our lives, Isaac and Rebekah encounter painful issues. They had fertility problems, so Issac prayed for God to open Rebekah's womb. God honored that prayer but, SURPRISE, He opened it up with twins! The two boys wrestled against each other, even in the womb.

Here is where Isaac and Rebekah diverge from their unified story: They chose favorites. Yep, Dad took Esau, the "rugged man's man," under his wing, and Rebekah pampered Jacob, the "mama's boy." The parents allowed their double blessing to divide them. The family struggled in strife from that point on. According to God, "two nations are in your womb, and two peoples will be separated from your body." (Genesis 25:23b)

FAITH JOURNEY

Lasting Consequences

Read Genesis 25:19-34: Esau and Jacob were always in conflict, even in the womb.

Read Genesis 27:1-43: The parents take sides, their terrible mistake.

Our families are not the first, nor the most messed up, and they will not be the last (until Christ comes back)! We can, however, be agents of change in the storyline of God's people. Through the rest of this season, we will work on ways to avoid Isaac and Rebekah's mistakes.

KEEPING THE FAMILY in unity is paramount for staying grounded during times of tumult. The instability caused by a family divided, especially when the husband and wife are not in harmony, is a recipe for a miserable life. Isaac and Rebekah's struggle has lasted for generations.

How we make our history write a better story for our future is by keeping unity with God's Word and our commitment to each other. When the season starts diverging from our comfort zone, it can be easy to respond as we witness others around us doing. Social media posts, in-person gossip, or fighting within the family or community are our natural human tendencies. But we must choose a revolutionary response: *Leading* in our new identities that flow with God's truth, not *following* the crowd. Like Jesus, we must be the example of servant love, which may cost us some discomfort or social standing.

This journey we are on matters. Our lives have an eternal impact on the human race. Our calling is to make sure others can see Christ as the loving savior He is. That is why we must choose a different path, the lesser-worn road. "The road less traveled" is a romantic sentiment; we all long to have the strength to choose that avenue. (*See "The Road Not Taken" by Robert Frost.*) Going in the opposite direction of the crowd takes a great deal of effort as well as courage, but in the end, it is worth the effort. While it may be challenging to live up to, Christian marriage should send shock waves through the communities we live in. Our human frailty may try to convince us to "just get along" and "not make waves." That is the easy path, the well-worn way. As Christians we are called to affect the world around us. We must make the most of the power entrusted to us. Witnessing the great pain and struggles around us should be enough to convince us to try.

As members of Christian marriages, we are to be salt and light to those around us, agents of change—not follow the world's virtues. Unfortunately, marriage within the Christian body is not immune from the misguided way of thinking. Misaligned families and marriages can be more like a soap opera than a reflection of our loving savior. Don't allow your union to be stained by lies that are designed to tear apart what God put together.

CURTIS' INPUT

Aligning Optics and Coming into Alignment with God's Will— Reflection & Refraction

For much of my career I have aligned optics to develop or improve telescopes. These telescopes typically consist of mirrors (reflectors) and lenses (refractors). Very nice, Curtis, but what can that possibly have to do with marriage and God?

Let's say I want to look closer at the moon, perhaps to see if there really is a man in the moon! So I design a telescope with a few lenses and a mirror, and some sort of tube that they all fit into. If I lay these special pieces out and look at the moon, cool as they may look by themselves, I have not done anything but have these telescope pieces lying around. But if I put them in their proper positions in the optical path, becoming one entity, I may be able to see the moon somewhat. But I cannot just put the optics in place without tweaking them to get a sharp image of the moon. Aligning optics takes time and patience. Each special optic not only has to be at the proper distance from each other; it cannot be tilted or off-center. Hence, considerable time and patience are required to achieve the objective.

Great! Now I have an idea about what the basics are to align a telescope. So what?

When you met your spouse, you may not have known their name and most certainly would not have known that they get irritated when you drink straight from the milk carton. There was no big plan most likely. But as soon as you get to know your future spouse, you become closer and see where your boundaries are and where theirs are. A plan starts to form. You start to put the pieces together, so to speak. Hopefully in the right order. You become one. But at first, your oneness is not that "perfectly aligned" relationship you want. There are little (and some not-so-little) tweaks that you need to become "perfect." With great care, God has developed a plan for you and your spouse. He wants your marriage perfectly in focus. If you read His word and put His plan first, your marriage follows His path. The tweaks throughout your marriage create a sharp image of God's love. Use the tools or pieces of the telescope that God has put out for you and your spouse to create a marriage that reflects God's love.

Living the Honeymoon Life

Curtis and I have chosen to answer the call from God to bring forth this message, the truth about marriage. When we were first married, our small group of couples would often tell us, "Enjoy it while it lasts. You won't be holding hands in five years."

When we were holding hands in five years, they said, "Just wait. Pretty soon you won't want to be in the same room too long together."

When we attempted to spend every moment in the same room together after 10 years, they said, "Just wait. The romance dies once you stop looking so young."

When we stopped looking so young, the romance was alive and well. . . and they stopped giving us advice.

WITHIN THE CHURCH, we need to be the trendsetters: only positive spouse-building conversations and a higher expectation of what this alliance should look like within the Christian community. As Curtis says, "You're on the same team!"

I challenge you, and myself, the next time we are in fellowship and the conversation is anything but spouse-building to: take the lead, point the way. Say something like, "I know it's easy to find fault with the person you are with so often, but aren't we glad God doesn't dwell on our shortcomings?" That usually is gentle enough to redirect the conversation, at least while you are around. After a while, people start to change their words around you. Then it becomes a new habit for them: Your principles are reinforced within them, causing their minds to be renewed, birthing positive conversations.

Be the change! Put a higher standard on your marriage. Keep the unity and peace in your relationship. It is the plan God has for you as the example of his Bride of Christ. God is inviting you and your spouse into participating in the final greatest act of human history: the marriage of the Lamb to His church. But it is our responsibility to behave in a way to present ourselves bright and clean. Our unity, agreement, and peace make way for God's calling and love to work through us. We cannot represent the Prince of Peace if our marriages are a war zone.

But can we bring the Kingdom of Heaven here on earth as Jesus taught? (*See Matthew 6:10*) Jesus teaches us to ask for heaven to be reflected and lived out in the here and now. I am of the belief that this includes our most sacred human covenant, Holy Matrimony.

SPRING

Recipe for a Strong Marriage

The Story of the Coffee Bean

CONSIDER THIS:

- Pour some water into a pot. Bring it to a boil. Add a potato. Allow the potato to remain in the boiling water for 15 minutes.
- Pour some water into a pot. Bring it to a boil. Add an egg to it. Allow the egg to remain in the boiling water for 15 minutes.
- Pour some water into a pot. Bring it to a boil. Add a coffee bean to it. Allow the coffee bean to remain in the boiling water for 15 minutes.

What happened to the potato? It became soft. What happened to the egg? It became hard.

What happened when you put in the coffee bean? It remained intact, but it changed the water around it.

All three of these were subjected to the same circumstance for the same amount of time. Why was the outcome so much different? Because of what each was made of. Today, as a couple, commit to being the coffee bean in every environment and circumstance you find yourself in. Don't allow the surroundings to determine what you become. Change the atmosphere where God has planted you for the better! (Gordon, Jon and West, Damon, *The Coffee Bean*)

Eternal Return on Efforts in Marriage

Read 2 Corinthians 11:2: Paul uses the analogy of marriage to represent the relationship of Christians to Christ, as a pure virgin.

Ephesians 5:27: Why husbands are called to love their wives as Christ loves the Church—to cleanse her.

Revelation 19:7-8: Christ returns to take His Bride, the Church, who has made herself ready—bright and clean.

What does this mean for eternity?

Scripture promises a final reunion when Christ comes back to unite with His Bride, the Church. We are not ready and Holy by our nature; we allow the work of Christ through the Holy Spirit to get in and cleanse us. Then we are coffee beans—or as Jesus calls us, salt and light—to the community around us. We model what Christ has done so others are able to make changes in their marriages because of our witness. The amount of love and holiness and getting ready that we do within our marriage, and subsequently our family, has an eternal value! Go and love your spouse!

The Story of the Apple—Lack of Leadership and Honor

Let's review a familiar story. We start with this perfectly unified pair, Adam and Eve. They are set loose in a perfect environment, and God said, "From any tree of the garden you may freely eat; but from the tree of the knowledge of good and evil you shall not eat, for on the day that you eat from it you will certainly die" (Genesis 2:16b-17). There was an abundance of "yeses" regarding which food could be eaten and only one "no."

It could be that Adam received the command before Eve had been fashioned. Perhaps Adam would have had to share with Eve what God had commanded. I would imagine it was discussed in the walks in the cool of the day with God. But whether she received it firsthand or not, somehow Eve started to misquote and rewrite the command. By the time the serpent entered the scene, Eve had probably already thought very much about the tree. Eve may have already wandered around the tree many times. Perhaps it had become the center of her attention. The tree in the "center of the garden" was among hundreds of trees that could be eaten from, yet Eve was focused on the tree of knowledge. When challenged by the serpent, she misquotes the command by adding "or touch it." (Genesis 3:3b) (Sorry, sister, that one is on you.) This addition gave room for the crafty serpent to cause her to question God.

And where is Adam during this exchange? He was with her. In their first challenge together, they did not operate within the original design God had intended. Adam did not take his rightful place as spiritual leader, and Eve did not honor her husband. The Word of God records for us, "she took some of its fruit and ate; and she also gave *some* to her husband with her, and he ate." (Genesis 3:6b)

God's original intent for this couple was that they work and play side by side and be fruitful and multiply—to add to what God had started. They had a great opportunity to cooperate and submit to God's perfect plan. But Eve, Adam, and the serpent chose to disobey the only command—thus destroying peace and unity in Eden—and we are all still living the curse today.

Phoebe's No-Bake Cookie Obsession

LIKE THESE DELICIOUS but simple no-bake cookies, getting the dating habit up and running does not need to be a black-tie occasion. What is important is that it is consistent and accessible every day. Like this recipe demonstrates, by tying together seven common ingredients, one pan, and a few measuring utensils, you have a decadent dessert. It helps to remember the adage KISS (Keep It Simple, Stupid).

Phoebe's No-Bake Cookie Obsession

2 cups white sugar

½ cup butter

¾ cup milk (we use whole)

⅓ cup unsweetened cocoa powder

Wax paper to fit cookie sheet

⅔ cup peanut butter (smooth)

2 teaspoons vanilla extract

3 cups oats + 1 pinch

1. Place wax paper on a cookie sheet.
2. Combine sugar, butter, milk, and cocoa (using a fine mesh strainer and sifting cocoa through with a spoon helps ensure that no clumps form with the cocoa) in a large saucepan.
3. Cook over medium-low heat, stirring constantly until the mixture comes to a rolling boil. Will take 3 to 4 minutes.
4. Remove from heat. Cool 1 minute.
5. Add peanut butter and vanilla. Stir to blend.

6. Add oats and stir well to coat evenly. If the mixture looks too dry, add a splash of milk, then stir to mix.

7. Quickly drop heaping spoons of mixture onto wax paper.

8. Cool completely (if you can wait). Store in a cool, dry place.

Some of us really like chocolate, and some like peanut butter. The combination of the two might light your taste buds up! When you combine yummy peanut butter with delicious chocolate, it creates a new, single mouthwatering masterpiece. This can be your marriage.

A Recipe for a Strong Marriage

During Spring season, changes happen such as moving, the birth of a child, changing careers or jobs, empty-nesting, and reversing roles with aging parents. The temptation can be to let the marriage take a back seat. But keeping the freshness intact and rediscovering each other, making "us" a priority even when time and energy demands are high, ensures we don't lose sight of the most important commitments: God and our marriage. We think it is an exciting challenge to steal away, just you and your spouse, not allowing the demanding world around you to keep you distant from one another.

Like personal preferences in food tastes, each of us has a preferred love language—the flavor of preference for affection and love we hunger for. If you and your spouse do not know each other's love languages, take the simple and free test at:

https://5lovelanguages.com/quizzes/love-language

It is important to learn and speak or work in your spouse's specific language. This is what we call "filling the love tank." When preparing for big changes associated with Spring, it is important to fill the love tank before entering this season. Curtis and I like to think of it as making deposits into an account so when the inevitable withdrawal is needed—like forgetting or minimizing an important event for your spouse—the deficit is not so deep. But the deposits must be in the currency most valuable to the receiver, the account holder.

Perhaps you are a "physical touch" speaker, and your spouse is a "quality time" hearer. One way to satisfy both languages is to set out a simple picnic on a blanket, in a quiet spot. Pack no-bake cookies, sandwiches, and homemade lemonade. Lie on the blanket, feeding each other a bite or two. Once you've finished eating, lie back and hold hands while enjoying the quiet. Add in a devotional or some worship music to keep the focus on your heavenly lover as well.

Living the Honeymoon Life

When planning your dates and sabbaths together, take inventory of each other's favorite love tank deposits. For Curtis, I know that a quiet evening together, like just taking in the stars up on our lookout deck, is a true tank filler. Curtis brings my coffee to me in bed every day. Efforts like these are inexpensive yet high-return habits that take your marriage from the doldrums and routine to a honeymoon life.

WITH THIS SMALL, one-hour investment, you have made deposits in each other's love tank to get ready for the pressure that the changes in life bring. It is a good idea whenever changes can be anticipated that you take the time to stock up on deposits in the love account. Think of it as a rainy-day fund.

Likewise, utilizing love tank deposits with our Heavenly Father causes peace and joy to reign in our lives. Remember, King David was a ruler; he had power, prestige, and a harem, and yet his greatest passion was for his Heavenly Father. Psalm 42:1 says, "As the deer pants for the water brooks, so my soul pants for you, O God." You can hear the desperation in his words. He can't live without drinking in the goodness of God. He cannot survive outside of communion with his Redeemer. Staying hungry and thirsty for the things of God—first in our lives—puts our hearts right toward the second highest desire, our spouse. It just follows that we want to honor his or her needs.

FUN & GAMES

Going Old School

STOP. PLAY NOW. *Connect the Dots*

Each of you should pick a different-colored pen. I am always green; it is my favorite color. On the dot grid above, one of you starts the game by drawing a line to connect two of the dots. It can be horizontal or vertical, not diagonal. The object is to complete squares. When you complete one, write your initials in it. The player with the most initials wins. Besides, it makes for a very colorful page. I say if you win, save that victory as a "get-out-of-jail free" pass to get out of a future task or forgive an infraction. LOL!

Another portable and simple example is Mancala, an ancient game for two players where each player attempts to capture the most pieces possible. It is a perfect set-up to chat and look at each other because the board orientation requires that you face each other.

Newer on the scene at only 700 years old is Farkle. Using six dice, each player attempts to be the first to amass a score of 10,000 points by die combinations and values. Again, you are facing each other as you play, and we choose to cheer for each other to win. Both games require little set-up and few pieces. Curtis and I carry a bag of six dice in each of our cars so if the occasion arises and we need a game to play we are ready; and trust me, it happens in our lives. Curtis and I like to keep score; we have a scorebook for many of our games to have bragging rights later. These are fun ways to make sure you keep play in your marriage.

SPRING

Fresh Starts and Do-Overs

SALT AND LIGHT

Minister to the Ministering

Curtis and I are called to minister to those who are ministering.

Whatever your gifting, the opportunity to be salty and shiny is at your fingertips every day. Committing to what you can do today is better than waiting for what you might do one day.

One of our marriage callings has been to pray for the pastors whom God has brought into our lives—past, present, and future. We had a season of hosting groups of missionaries and evangelists from around the world to soften our hearts to all those who lay down their lives in full-time ministry. That has confirmed our bucket list ministry: to establish a sabbatical ministry in which full-time men and women of God and their families can take a much-needed vacation. We envision it being all-expenses paid, all arrangements handled. While we have not broken ground on this mission, we have watched God bring people to our lives that we know are a piece of the puzzle that will make this calling a reality.

While change happens all around us at lightning speed, our firm grasp on a shared calling will bind us together. With a clear picture of what you are called to accomplish and where you are headed, you can remain steadfast, holding to this anchor even during the discomfort of changes. Keeping your eye on your mutual purpose and vision helps to maintain the sense of unity. You are building a legacy in the tradition and glory of God your Father.

Coleslaw

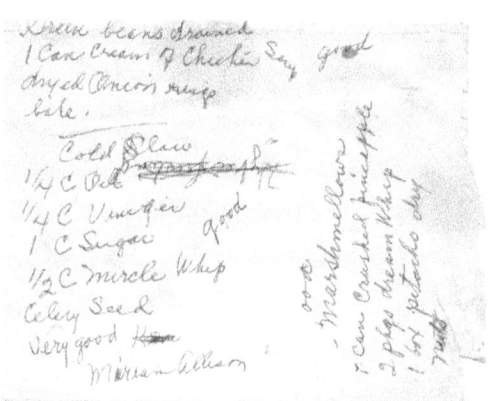

When I was a child, we spent every Mother's Day with my mom and both grandmothers. We always picked up a bucket of Kentucky Fried Chicken and had a picnic at the lake. This handwritten recipe is the closest thing you can find to our "takeout," and it has been made at most family functions all of my life. Doing it right, and the same way it has been done, has created a legacy within my family. If something as trivial as a coleslaw recipe can create a legacy, just think what honoring small habits to keep the marriage spicy could do!

THINK OF THE memorization verse in this chapter. If husband and wife are in Christ, your marriage is a new creation *daily*. Forget past scores and set your eyes on Jesus' dream for what your marriage will look like every day, long into the future.

SPRING

Krupp Marriage Experience

Making the Honeymoon Last—
I Surrender One-Tenth

PRACTICING FAITH THROUGH tithing is one of the arenas that reveals our hearts. Perhaps you have heard people make rationalizations or legal arguments about how and when to tithe: "Should you tithe before tax amount?" "Should you tithe to your local church?" "The New Testament does not say to tithe." No, it doesn't—Jesus says to give it all!

The best rule for tithing is: Do it. Whatever the Lord puts on your heart, give it.

Tithing, like the Sabbath, is for your good. It builds your faith and provides an opportunity for God to show up with provision. Money is a renewable resource; you can always make more of it. Training our faith through money is a safe place to stretch our faith wings.

Add tithing to your marriage mission. Ask God to reveal ways to give of your increase and watch it multiply. Tithing is not giving to get, but you will be amazed at how God shows up when you test Him in giving. (*See Malachi 3:10*)

CURTIS' INPUT

Tithing—Trust God

When we moved to Sigourney, Iowa, in the summer of 1995, we started going to church regularly. I came from the school of "put what you can in" when the plate is passed around. A little, back then, was anywhere from $2 to maybe $15. But the Lord challenges you sometimes, and this was the first challenge of faith for our little family.

At the time I was working for McLeodUSA Telecom as a fiber-optic locator, making about $10.60/hour; not even $2,000/month unless I got overtime. The position was considered part-time temporary when I first started.

I think it was after Christmas when I decided to jump out in faith and told Terri that I think we should consistently give $15/week as our offering. She was always supportive of this and said that I should do what I felt was right. She felt the money pinch worse than anyone but never complained. A month or so later, my position became part-time permanent, which meant I was guaranteed at least 30 hours/week, even in the winter. This came at a good time because I wasn't working that much and was looking at joining my in-laws' insurance company. FYI, I am not a salesman.

So, I said to Terri, I think we should up our offering to $20/week, and she encouraged me again, "Do what the Lord guides you to give." A month or two later, I was given a clothing allowance at my job.

I was feeling a connection here and decided to give the entire tithe! Terri's response: "You can't out-give God." We started tithing, and by summer I received a great raise (to about $12.50/hour), and my position became full-time permanent. God wanted my family all in, not just dipping my toes in the water. And that is how the Krupps came to tithe—and it has been that way since.

Change Is Not Always Negative—We Are Still Learning and Growing

AFTER ALL THESE decades together, there is still no one I would rather spend my time with than my husband. Why is that? Why has our marriage been an outlier?

One factor may be that we approach our marriage as a friendship, a partnership, and our ministry. Early on and throughout each season, we have talked honestly about our long-term relationship. (Heck, we have talked about what the impact of our marriage will be after we are gone.) We take into account our faith, finances, and children.

For example, early on we knew we wanted children, and we knew we wanted one of us to be a full-time parent. Since Curtis had a clear professional vision, I was the best candidate to be the housewife. Reverse engineering, with an end goal firmly established, ensures your marriage stays on track. Knowing where we want to be in the future will tell us which direction to go each day, in order to get there. While we did not and still do not have all the answers, we have a foundation in Christ so that when we get off course, we have our true north, Jesus, to align with daily.

Keeping the Important First

To keep a rhythm of connectedness, fill out a calendar of your commitments to each other. Put solid boundaries in place that are non-negotiables; devotions, prayer, date night, keeping outsiders out of your business, making the world wonder if there really can be that much happiness in this life. Yes, there is, and you can have it—and they can too!

Include:

- Daily devotions and prayer together: Walk in the cool of the day in the presence of God. (*See Genesis 3:8a*) If you are not already in the habit of doing devotions or reading scripture together, a simple way to start is on the Bible App. The devotional can be done separately at a time convenient to each of you. You both can comment on the passage to keep each other tuned in to thoughts on the verses and their impact on you. To start the habit of prayer together, make a prayer list and take turns saying the prayer out loud. Having a record to document answered prayers encourages the habit.

- Weekly Sabbath: "Jesus said to them, 'The Sabbath was made for man, not man for the Sabbath.'" (Mark 2:27) Choose whichever day of the week works best for you both. We like to go from evening to evening. Remove all menial and unpleasant tasks. Do not be legalistic but enjoy the rest carved out for you and your spouse.

- Monthly date night that is on the calendar. Utilize the QR code to print out a ticket or make your own to make sure this formal calendar event is set in stone. Knowing you are the top priority in your spouse's agenda can really turn the romantic fire back on. "The husband must fulfill his duty to his wife, and likewise also the wife to her husband." (1 Corinthians 7:3)

- Yearly escape to refresh, reconnect, and relax. They can be stay-cations to extended holidays abroad, use your creativity and stay on budget to make these blessings.

The key is to prioritize your time with the Lord and with each other. You will need to check back in frequently to see how you are doing and adjust anything that is not working.

We celebrated our thirty-fourth anniversary and are making plans for something special to mark the thirty-fifth. But in between now and then, you better believe we are making little celebrations every day!

For I am confident of this very thing, that He who began a good work among you will complete it by the day of Christ Jesus.

PHILIPPIANS 1:6

Living the Honeymoon Life

On July 7, 2022, at Grace Church Maui, David MacDonald delivered a beautiful prophecy that confirmed many of the words of knowledge and promises that God had given us over the past several decades.

Curtis and I were already confident that God would faithfully see His promises come to pass, but to have words delivered through a total stranger, speaking to exactly who we were and what skills God had already put in us to bring it about, was, well, miraculous.

We recorded the message while we were receiving it. Since then, we have listened to it frequently to keep the truth in the front of our minds and hearts and to squash and expose any circumstances and lies that attempt to come between us and our calling.

If you have promises that God has given you, write them down. Make a record of what He has already said and done, so when you need reminding, it is there to testify.

The Weather Is Heating Up!

We have experienced it every time we have moved, and in each stage of our ever-growing family, change is difficult. The uncertainty of what's to come and what will be left behind can be overwhelming prospects for a marriage.

By setting in place daily habits that focus your marriage on God, speaking the language your spouse longs to hear, and prioritizing your time together, the uncertainty becomes just another chapter in your story.

Having a firm grasp on navigating Spring changes, we can set our sights on the busyness associated with Summer. The long days filled with obligations need to be tamed and controlled. Ensuring that your marriage is safe from over-commitment and hectic schedules will take boundaries and discipline. In the next season, we will explore the building blocks that ensure every yes is worth all the noes it will cost.

Happy Honeymooning!

SUMMER

HUMMINGBIRDS

Hummingbirds are the best example of sugar junkies in nature. When I put up my feeders, I fear that I am contributing to the obesity of the species. With their quick, constant motion and fast-flapping wings, they are a spectacle to observe. Most varieties of hummingbirds around the globe have perfectly developed beaks for nectar retrieving, but biologists have discovered that in South America, some varieties sport beaks that are better suited for fighting than food collection. It is theorized that the conditions in the jungle demand more ammunition to fend off predators for food and female rights, which means that birds are less fit for eating than fighting. I don't consider that progress.

Summer—Too Busy to Stop and Eat from the Roses

Hummingbirds are beautiful and curious creatures. Some true facts about hummingbirds: They can fly backward. They migrate solo for up to 500 miles at a time. They have no sense of smell but great vision (research shows they can be trained to recognize individual faces). They can consume up to double their body weight in nectar per day.

They are said to have meaning when sighted, like a good omen or an inspiration of hope. I don't subscribe too much to those sentiments but watching two little hummers compete over the same feeding receptacle when six more are available does give me great delight.

It brings to mind a spectacle that I myself have participated in. If I see someone being successful and enjoying what they are doing in their calling, I may try to step into that identity or role for myself.

I will emulate what they are doing, thinking it must be good because they are having success with it. But the truth is I should celebrate that person's success and learn what I can from it. I need to speak in my own authentic voice and share what has been uniquely planted in me instead. There are lots of places to impart my gifts, and the world is brighter when I shine my own light.

This can be true in marriages. You see friends' social media posts of their wonderful vacations, their youthful bodies, and their seemingly idyllic family and think, *Wow, we should be like them.* I remember going through a bit of covetousness myself as our teenagers struggled mightily. While other parents were celebrating all the accolades and honors their children were achieving, we were just trying to keep everyone alive and out of jail. What had we done wrong?

For my part, I had taken my eyes off of my own provision. I had allowed someone else's success and blessings to cause me to compare my situation to theirs, and I risked wasting the season God was bringing me through. I was not being kept from blessings; it was that I had my own path to traverse and my own testimony to write. God was answering my prayers and giving me signs of hope everywhere, like a little hummingbird showing up at my feeders.

Rest is not idleness, and to lie sometimes on the grass under trees on a summer's day, listening to the murmur of the water, or watching the clouds float across the sky, is by no means a waste of time.

JOHN LUBBOCK, *THE USE OF LIFE*

SUMMER

The Season

Be the Encourager

I grew up in a family with seven kids. I was the youngest, or the "baby," or the most spoiled one. It didn't feel that way. I read somewhere, long ago, that the oldest is the overachiever and the youngest is the most fun or easygoing. That is mostly true: my oldest brother, Dave, definitely would be considered an overachiever, but I think my brother Scott would be voted most fun in our family (He is two years older than me.).

As a kid, I looked up to all of my siblings. In fact, I strived to be like them more than they knew. I loved playing sports, so I was very competitive. Naturally, I wanted to outdo my siblings if I tried something they did. In baseball, brother Gene was the gold standard for me. He was fast—REALLY fast. And he could hit the ball. He was always at the top of the batting average list no matter what level he played. I loved watching him play. Even after I would play a game in Little League, my dad would ask if I wanted to be dropped off at home or go with him to Gene's Senior League game. My dad was his coach. I would go every time to see him play. It was like watching a Major League game for me, and I was close to the action. The level of play that Gene's team played was something I could hardly wait to attain.

During my last season of Little League, I finally cracked the top ten on the batting average list, just not as high as Gene. It was on display on some bulletin board at the fields. I turned to my dad all proud and he already knew. He was beaming.

Then I asked him, "Do you think I will ever be as good of a hitter as Gene?" His smile vanished. He didn't realize I was chasing my brother.

"Curt," he said, "what are you talking about? As long as Gene hits the ball on the ground, he's probably going to get to first base as a minimum. He has a natural eye for the ball and amazing speed. In some ways, you are better than him. You hit home runs and long drives into the outfield. You have a natural eye for the ball like Gene, and very good speed, but you have great power. Don't ever think you are less of a player than Gene. You both have great gifts—they are just different."

If you haven't realized it, my dad was the most inspirational man I have ever known. He was our great encourager. God also addresses our gifts and talents. He wants us to utilize the gifts he gave us. If someone inspires you to better use those gifts, they are good examples, but your gifts are your own. Use them to God's glory.

Scripture to Memorize Together

And he (Jesus) said to them 'Come away by yourselves to a secluded place and rest awhile.' (For there were many people coming and going, and they did not even have time to eat.)

MARK 6:31

LIKE THE HUMMINGBIRD, I have been guilty many times of seasons of hurry. They are almost always accompanied by seasons of worry. To learn the obedience of slowing down and noticing the blessings we already have is not natural to me, but it is exactly what Jesus modeled in His time on earth.

When our children were young, I loved the days of just allowing them to look at bugs or dig in the sand or play with the Jackson's chameleons that populated our yard. It was magical and a great reminder of how much detail and whimsy God wove into His creation. Research is catching up with our fast-paced lives, showing that children who are bored develop creativity, valuable skills, and self-esteem.[5] Like children we must embrace "boredom" at times to catch the wonder that is right under our nose.

Hurry + Worry = Fury

Does it sometimes feel like everyone around you has gone mad? The noise of daily life can be overwhelming. The loud, aggressive voices of everything are counter to Godliness. The *do what feels good* philosophy, or "cancel culture," just gets so loud and moves so fast that we start to see and believe that we are the only one still believing and holding to God's immutable truths. That is exactly what the prince of darkness needs you to believe.

The reality is that all around us are fellow believers, angels warring on our behalf (*See Daniel 10: 8-14*) and the Holy Spirit full of power within us (*See John 16:7*) Greater is he who is in you. (*See 1 John 4:4*) But it is difficult to live in that truth when we are surrounded by such a loud clamor of opposition and opportunity. From the White House down to the schoolhouse, sometimes even within the church house, culture looks to be flowing away from God and Truth.

My eyes were opened to this phenomenon one day as I drove aggressively, jockeying for position to be ahead of the traffic. When I uttered those words, "No one knows how to drive on this road but me!" At that very moment I looked over into the "slow lane" and a woman about my age was driving the speed limit. She was smiling and focused on the road. Was I really in that big of a rush? Did a car length here or there really gain me that much advantage? No, I was competing only within myself. I safely merged right and stayed in the slow lane, driving the speed limit all the way to work. I arrived a minute or two late, but I had peace and was in a mindset to be able to teach.

I attempt to stay in the slow lane now, in all my life's activities. I try to observe those around me and allow for others' errors. It is amazing how much you "see" when you are driving the speed limit in the slow lane. Summer and its endless obligations and opportunities, long hours of sunlight and fun in the sun, can cause us to rush and hurry through with blinders on. It is imperative that we slow our roll and pay attention as we maneuver the path of Summer.

Now when the attendant of the man of God had risen early and gone out, behold, an army with horses and chariots was circling the city. And his servant said to him, 'This is hopeless, my master! What are we to do?' And he said, 'Do not be afraid, for those who are with us are greater than those who are with them.' Then Elisha prayed and said, 'Lord, please, open his eyes so that he may see.' And the Lord opened the servant's eyes, and he saw; and behold, the mountain was full of horses and chariots of fire all around Elisha.

2 KINGS 6:15-17

Shark's Cove—Yikes!

When we lived in Oahu, one of our favorite spots was Shark's Cove on the north shore. It has a shallow, rocky lagoon teeming with small reef creatures (crustaceans, fish, sea slugs, etc.) There is also a cove, of course (Never did I see a shark there!) and a large formation of lava rock that protects the lagoon. Typically, I would hang with the family for a short period, exploring the lagoon, and then Terri would see my antsy behavior and send me off to do the adventurous things that call to me. These included rock jumping, exploring underwater caves, diving as deep as I could without risking my life, and searching for large reef creatures. Both of us would tell people about the wonderful family destination of Shark's Cove. The variety of amazing sea life was comparable only to the more tourist-visited Hanauma Bay on the south shore.

The thing I didn't get while we were telling people about this aquatic wonderland was that Terri and I were talking about two separate parts of the same place. She spent more time with the kids in the lagoon, and I spent more time on the rocks and in the cove. One of the last times we were there, after I had my fun, Terri said, "It's high tide." I thought, well that is wonderful. . . A little help here. . . "Can you help me with the kids as we explore the lagoon?" I had satisfied my adventurous side, so why not enjoy some of this "boring" lagoon stuff? This particular lagoon experience was unforgettable. We saw our typical fish variety: butterflyfish, goatfish, damselfish, tangs, gobies, triggers, etc. The reefs were full of urchins, corals, some starfish, and sea cucumbers. As we slowly moseyed around the reefs, there were gleeful shouts from our children as they found less common sightings. One time one of the kids said, "I found an octopus!" Another time: "Hey, there is an eel!" Yet another time: "Look over here. . . CLEANER SHRIMP!" It seemed like new discoveries would never end.

The discoveries were fantastic. But the biggest takeaway was seeing my children light up. This was the part Terri is talking about when describing Shark's Cove. This was the "boring" part of it for me. I have learned that taking time to slow down is an important way to not miss all that He has for you.

Embrace the Shake—What I Learned from Yoga About Being a Christian

ONE OF MY healthy habits is practicing yoga. (There is yoga that espouses a religious belief and misrepresents the origin of breath, but remember, God's first act with man was to breathe life into him. I practice the exercise, not a spiritual aspect.) One of the insights that I have gained from yoga is that "we are always practicing." That is, we are never finished learning. In fact, in yoga it is expected that you will push yourself beyond your comfort level in each pose in order to progress. The atmosphere lends itself to focusing primarily on the moment and the pose that you are currently undertaking. There is no room to mourn or regret past shortcomings, only a new breath for the new challenge. In yoga shaking is not only acceptable, but also the gauge by which growth is measured.

The yoga studio I practice at has a very common statement: "Embrace the shake." If we as Christians adopted this mindset in our faith walk, we would be a lot bolder when given the opportunity to witness. We would give more generously and undertake challenging opportunities because we know that Jesus, our master Teacher, is right there in the practice with us, ensuring we don't fall too hard. "Embrace the shake" encourages us to give it our best shot, no matter whether we feel confident, prepared, or particularly skilled in the moment.

In yoga, there is also the demand for setting aside everything but the current challenge—to focus and be in the moment of your practice to the exclusion of all other worries. The peace and stillness created by being in the moment facilitates the expansion of physical growth.

In our Christian Walk, turning our focus on the Kingdom first helps us to be available when opportunities present themselves, no matter what circumstances are going on around us. When Jesus said, "Come away with me by yourselves to a secluded and quiet place," it was at the height of the ministry, as the disciples did not even have time to eat. Jesus calls us to prioritize rest and spending time alone with Him.

While practicing yoga, modifiers are presented for each pose, either to reduce or increase the difficulty. For example, you may need to start with your knee on the floor for side plank. You may shake and tremble as you hold this challenging pose. Even if you modify the pose, sometimes you will fall out of it. As Christians we need to live in a community where it's okay to shake a little as long as we're growing and behaving as followers of Jesus, living and loving His way.

Church should be the safest place to shake and fall, not the place we feel most judged. A place to stretch ourselves outside of our comfort zone even if it doesn't look pretty. What if we come along a single mom in our neighborhood who is struggling just to get by. We can watch her kids and give her the night off. What if we sit with the widow who attends church alone and invite her to lunch once a month. Nothing extravagant. We are already going to eat anyway. We are just expanding our circle to include those who don't have the safety net they need. These opportunities will come when we get to know Jesus and learn to be like Him as we honor our quiet time in prayer and God's Word. Only after we focus our attention on His Kingdom will we find the strength to step out in action. Are we prepared for the ministry God is laying in our path? There's only one way to find out and that's to "embrace the shake" and walk with Jesus!

Living the Honeymoon Life

I understand that there is passion and energy on both sides of the conversation when it comes to yoga. There are without a doubt religiously held beliefs associated with yoga. I personally have been warned that yoga is directly accredited to the devil. But that is just not scriptural. God is the author of ALL things! The devil's only credit is to pervert and deceive people about his authority over things. Yes, he is allowed to reign in this world for a time, but he has never created anything. On my side, I give glory to God and pray and worship as I perform the exercises. (Consider Job 1:7: Satan answers to God, period!)

If the topic of yoga is painful to you, please know I respect and love your heart. This book has no intention of changing anyone's beliefs about yoga. My message is that it all belongs to God; use it to His glory. But if that is a stumbling block in your life—let's say you used to subscribe to the spiritual angle of yoga—let me be the first to support your decision to avoid this topic and section.

Like everything in living a Honeymoon Life, we must come at it knowing God is the ultimate authority, and He will walk with us exactly where we are on our path to get us to the final destination: heaven.

 **FAITH JOURNEY**

Peter Walks on Water...
Well, for a Moment

See Matthew 14:22-32

The disciples had gotten into a boat to cross the sea and Jesus stayed behind to dismiss the crowd. Jesus caught up to them by walking on the water. Assuming He was a ghost, they cried out in fear, but Jesus comforted them, saying, "Take courage, it is I, do not be afraid."

Peter challenged Him by saying, "Lord, if it is you, command me to come to You on the water." I am thinking, *Peter, how many people have you seen walking on water? Of course it's Jesus!*

Like Peter, even when Jesus answers my prayer, I may need further confirmation. But our gentle Jesus honored Peter's request and said, "Come!"

Peter got out of the boat and took steps toward Jesus. But then he focused on the waves and wind, so he sank. He cried out, "Lord, save me!" And Jesus did.

Often in the telling of this story, Peter is criticized for sinking. But think about it; there were at least eleven other disciples in the boat who could not even muster the faith or courage to attempt to walk toward Jesus on the water. I think Jesus was so patient and gracious because He never expected Peter to walk all the way to Him on the water; just the "shake" of the attempt showed tremendous faith.

It's not how far you walk to Jesus. It's the getting out of the boat that proves faith.

Who Am I in Christ?

Making of a Human Being

MAKING A "HUMAN being" out of a "human doing" requires a great deal of discipline. I struggle in this area mightily. I am very productivity motivated. I am a list maker and find absolute joy in checking off the boxes. Accomplishing tasks brings such a sense of value for me. But we are not designed to live in an endless loop of tasks. We need to live in our identity in Christ and our inherent value as the image of God.

In the Garden of Eden, Adam and Eve are set in charge of the creation. "God blessed them; and God said to them, 'Be fruitful and multiply, and fill the earth, and subdue it; and rule over the fish of the sea and over the birds of the sky and over every living thing that moves on the earth.'" (Genesis 1:28) This job was meant to be a blessing. God placed them in the garden to continue building up creation in the manner that He had begun. To learn and live within but over the environment in which Adam and Eve were placed; not to be slaves and servants to their environment, but to utilize it and bring fruit from it.

While the activities of a human "doing" may look like we are living up to the charge, the mindset is very different. If I value myself by what I do instead of the fact that I am the image of my creator, then I miss the reason I was created in the first place. God needs nothing from me; He is omnipotent. The fulfillment of my calling is to grow me and to allow me to be more in His image as I participate in the work at hand.

If a day comes, due to injury or illness or age, that I am unable to "do" what I once did, am I less fruitful in God's plan? Not if I cling fast to my true identity. I am created in the image of my Heavenly

Father and called to live in the blessing in which He has set me, to reflect His creative essence.

If you feel stuck in the cycle of valuing yourself because of your works, take a moment and look at the blessing your Father intends for you to live in. You are loved and worthy just by *being* you!

> Then God said, 'Let us make man in Our image, according to Our likeness, and let them rule over the fish of the sea and over the birds of the sky and over the birds of the sky and over the cattle and over all the earth, and over every creeping thing that creeps on the earth.'
>
> **GENESIS 1:26**

The Jesus Way

Remember Jesus' invitation to "come away" came at the height of the ministry's effectiveness—or so the disciples thought. The Bible tells us that so many people were coming to them that they didn't have time to eat. (*See Mark 6:31b*) It would have seemed like the worst strategy to grow their organization. It would have gone against all of the SOPs (standard operating procedures) that they had in place. After all, isn't the great commission "Go into all the world and preach the gospel to all creation?" (Mark 16:15) Going into all the world would keep us very busy. Doing it Jesus' way, one opportunity of kindness at a time, we do not get overwhelmed; we find peace.

> Trust in the Lord with all your heart, and do not lean on your own understanding. In all your ways acknowledge Him, and He will make your paths straight.
>
> **PROVERBS 3:5-6**

Counterfeit: Spotting the Fake; Reclaiming God's Design

Professionals who are trained to spot counterfeit money do so by studying genuine currency. They memorize the look and feel of every detail of the authentic bill so that if a fraud is passed along, it will be detected. In my search to ensure that this was indeed the practice, I encountered a website from the Secret Service on how to spot counterfeit bills, and you guessed it, it was a study of the details of legitimate currency.[6]

One of the great deceptions has been the counterfeit of God's design for marriage. It has come in many forms. I am not only referring to political and social issues like same-sex or living together outside of marriage. Within our Christian marriages, we seem to carry a lack of understanding of what our roles should be and how our calling is built into our union. The phrase "the honeymoon doesn't last" is spread even in the Christian community and it is counter to God's plan for marriage.

God designed Eden as a place of constant community. There was fruitful work to be done but no labor. Adam and Eve were fully confident and secure walking around naked. God himself would spend time in the garden communing with them. That is the full design of how our marriages should run, sharing complete intimacy and communion with God and each other. We are meant to enjoy closeness with each other, working side-by-side to create and cultivate a beautiful environment.

So how do we get it so wrong? One problem we have in our society is overcommitment too much busyness. It is like we are attempting to accomplish everything all at once. As my grandson observes as I work on my computer, "Oma, you have too many tabs open!" (LOL—out of the mouth of babes!) The drive to multitask and have too much on our plates causes even the most robust processor to slow and increase loading times.

Case study: Observe parents of young children in church. Have you seen them, ragged and worn? Often, they both hold full-time employment, the kids may each be in several activities, and then there's the pressure to serve in the church. (Curtis and I have been this family before.) This family does not have time or energy to commune in the garden with God or to enjoy the rest of God.

We are quick to fill our schedules and agendas with the busyness and activity that the world tells us we should value. When we do this, we counterfeit the call of our precious creator God, who longs to tarry in the garden with us.

How much different would our families, and especially our marriages, look if we stopped listening to the lies? What if we took God at His word and limited our activities and busyness to six days a week? What if we said "no" to some things that interrupted our intimacy with God and our spouses? Focusing on the most important task one at a time in order of necessity is actually the fastest way to accomplish more.

Perhaps like Curtis and me, you are beyond child-rearing years and wonder: What is your responsibility now? What if we changed the way we give away our time and became the example for our grown children? If we look back and see that we were completely wrong in our balance as we raised our children, we can apologize and admit our wrong. Perhaps their marriages and family life could better reflect God's design.

Challenge: Start today, looking at the list you created of all the activities you personally are committed to. Between you and your spouse, does tallying the list of obligations cause writer's cramp? If you still have school-age children in the house, consider their activities and commitments. If you didn't fill out the exercise earlier, fill out a one-week calendar, listing all of your combined commitments. Add up the number of minutes required to accomplish everything listed, including commute times. 8,640 are the total minutes in six days. If you include time to sleep and eat, not to mention your quiet time in the Lord, would an impossible scenario present itself?

If we are acting in faith, we realize that sometimes *not performing work* reminds us of our dependence on our Heavenly Father to provide for that day.

It is to be a Sabbath of solemn rest for you, *so that you may humble yourselves*; it is a permanent statute.

LEVITICUS 16:31 (EMPHASIS ADDED)

TRUE NORTH

With So Much on Our Plates, How Do We Make Time to "Come Away"?

That is why we have the Sabbath command. There will always be opportunities to "do," but our first priority is to "be" with Jesus. But how? We have been privileged to participate in many studies that tells us to do something but don't give us the how. Here are some ideas.

The first step is to make it a family (couple) priority. Just decide to do it. Second, choose a time on the calendar. If this is a new habit, try a short Sabbath. Perhaps on Sunday morning, cooperate worship and then enjoy an easy lunch and rest or quiet until early afternoon. Remember, you are practicing. Start where you are and make it doable. As you grow the habit, you will see the value and want to make it more intense. (Curtis and I are still, after thirty years of commitment to it, practicing our Sabbath.) The Sabbath is a blessing. It is not to be given too strict of interpretation or legal stranglehold on you. It is a part of your faith journey. (*See Mark 2:27.*)

If we say yes to everything, then nothing is given our full attention. Jesus taught that you would find treasure where your heart is. Reverse engineering will show us that if we look at our treasure, we will find out where our heart is.

Make a list of all the commitments that you and your spouse have. If you have children in the home, consider their schedules also.

His _____

_____

Hers _____

_____

Family/Ours _____

_____

Make a list of your hobbies and what you each enjoy doing.

His _____

_____

Hers _____

_____

Family/Ours _____

_____

Get out a calendar (Your phone works nicely; you seem to always have it with you), or you can print one (or maybe your bank still gives out free ones.)

If you calendar all of your commitments and hobbies, where does your Sabbath most easily fit in? Remember, we are embracing the shake and starting where we are. Once you find that spot, decide and commit to that time. If it's twelve hours, block twelve hours. The key is that nothing is allowed to interfere with that time. It is sacred, just like our work schedule is sacred.

CURTIS' INPUT

All Work, No Play

When we moved to Texas for my work at L3, I was excited because I was going back to working in a lab. It was going to be great not to be on the road away from my family. Well, part of that was correct. I wasn't on the road, but I was working a lot; typically, six days a week and ten hours a day. Not much time for family activities. I wasn't complaining; I was the only person trained to calibrate and repair sensors in this lab. The mission required my time, and Terri and I were good with that, for a while. But after a couple of years of it, it was a habit for me but a nuisance to my family. We didn't spend routine family time like we had before, and our family was showing signs of stress.

The bride of my youth came up to me one Sunday and asked a simple question: "Do you really need to work so much overtime still? I understand if you do, but the kids and I would really like to see you more. And we need to spend time together. Even if it's just every other weekend."

Talk about a gut punch. I was so busy enjoying the work at my hands that I forgot for whom I was doing that work. I stood there and thought about the question.

"You know?" I told her. "No, I don't have to work every weekend. I have caught up on the sensors, and I can just work it as I am truly needed, just like everyone else."

Work can be extremely gratifying, but we shouldn't forget to keep our true purpose at the forefront.

The Legal Side of Sabbath

One of the most blistering issues between Jesus and the Pharisees was the Sabbath. Jesus healed and walked and picked grain to eat on the Sabbath; these were violations of Jewish tradition. The command states not to do "work." So, did Jesus break the command of the Sabbath?

No. He did not work at his job (carpentry) or ask His disciples to fish. He healed the blind, caused the lame to walk, and freed those captive to ailments. Sounds like He acted in the loving nature of His heavenly Father, according to the prophecies of Isaiah. (*See Isaiah 35:4-6*)

Jesus performed seven healings on the Sabbath. It would appear that Jesus came to dismantle the myths that the synagogue officials had built around the Sabbath. He performed several of the healings in or around the temple, in front of the Pharisees. He knew that they were attempting to trick him or catch him doing something unlawful, but he was pointing out the hypocrisy of the institution and healing the Jewish tradition of its focus on *keeping* the Sabbath as opposed to *honoring* the Sabbath.

> Jesus said to them, "The Sabbath was made for man, not man for the Sabbath. So, the Son of Man is Lord even of the Sabbath."
>
> **MARK 2:27-28**

 FAITH JOURNEY

Jesus Heals Seven Times on the Sabbath

"Seven" in the Bible is the number of perfect completion and rest.

- **Luke 4:38-41**: After teaching at synagogue, He enters Peter's house and heals his mother-in-law.

- **Luke 6:6-10**: He heals in the synagogue the man with the withered hand.

- **Luke 13:10-17**: Again, in the synagogue, He heals the woman who was bent over for eighteen years.

- **Luke 14:1-6**: Attending a dinner party at a Pharisees' house, He heals the man with dropsy. He asked the leaders directly if it was legal to heal on the Sabbath.

- **Mark 1:21-28**: In the synagogue, He heals the man with the unclean spirit.

- **John 5:1-18**: At the pool of Bethesda, He heals the paraplegic and tells him to carry his pallet with him.

- **John 9:1-16**: Regarding the man born blind, Jesus used the opportunity to teach His disciples that infirmity is not always a matter of sin.

Jesus proves the heart of God the Father, showing it is ALWAYS the season to do good. Remember, it was legal to perform circumcision when the eighth day fell on the Sabbath. (*See John 7:23*) God loves to bring wholeness to His children, and so must we.

 **FUN & GAMES**

Practice Drowning Out the Noise

To spot the counterfeit within your relationship, you will need time and space to be united and comfortable with your spouse. The enemy of your soul attempts to convince you that you and your spouse are opposed to one another, but the truth is your spouse is your greatest ally, and together, you are a threat to his dominion. Getting into the habit of just enjoying creation together is a great start.

One of our favorite ways to accomplish this is to sit under the stars holding hands. Curtis and I recline on our cabana and take it all in. We open the Skyview® app on our phones. Or if you prefer, you can make up names to constellations. One I made up is "Lowly Worm," resembling Richard Scarry's illustrated character of the same name. It has two eyes and five stars that make an inchworm when connected.

Take time to just observe God, the maker of heaven and earth, who created all of this so you could see Him clearly. He loves to show His children the signs and wonders—if we can sit still long enough to pay attention

It can be difficult during the long summer days that stretch long hours of sunshine to appreciate that all the energy and fruit of this season must be intentionally invested so that when we face other seasons we are prepared. Our marriages in this busy season must carefully guard against forfeiting meaningful activity for busyness. While all marriages go through hectic times, learning to stay connected and on the same page even while feeling like we are ships passing in the night requires planning and a common purpose.

Ingredients—Yoked in Marriage, Work, and Mission

Aquila and Priscilla

IF YOU WANT to set the bar really high for completing the calling on your marriage, look no further than Priscilla and Aquila. Apparently, this couple taught Paul the trade of tent-making, which later helped him support himself. They were diligent stewards of the Way, the original title given to the early church. Acts 18:26 tells us while in Greece, they took Apollos into their home and "explained the way of God more accurately to him."

They hosted a home church and were mission trip companions to Paul. We know that they were protectors of Paul and the developing church, not allowing misinformation to find its way in. If you want a marriage mission statement, look at how Paul refers to this dynamic duo. Our marriages can have this kind of eternal impact.

"Greet Priscilla and Aquila, my fellow workers in Christ Jesus, who risked their own necks for my life, to whom not only I give thanks, but all the churches of the Gentiles, also greet also the church that meets at their house." (Romans 16:3-5a)

They are mentioned by name in Paul's letters to the Corinthians and Timothy, calling for them to be "greeted" or acknowledged. Clearly, Paul thought very highly of this couple, and they were an integral part of the early church. They were marketplace apostles, performing their service as they worked their trade. They are a prime example in the Bible of an impactful Christian marriage. How can we set our marriages apart and aspire to be more like Priscilla and Aquila (P&A)?

Finding Your Marriage Mission

Discovering your marriage mission is critical to living the Honeymoon Life. "With no vision, the people perish." (Proverbs 29:18a KJV) If we hope to be an example to others, we must be living it ourselves. God has called us to lead others to be their best. We must live out our God-given Marriage Missions daily. But we must first work to discover what our marriage mission is. If you have not yet taken the time to know what your common mission is, here is a place to start.

 **WORK IT OUT TOGETHER**

Life Missions

We recommend getting away for quiet time to do this. Spend time independently and corporately in prayer. Journal separately, then come together to brainstorm. You may use a Venn diagram or just his/her lists to identify the common responses.

Take time to list on paper or your phone all the things that you and your spouse naturally do together and enjoy (the work you just did on your calendar can help you identify some of these), like host get-to-gethers, get game nights arranged, volunteer at a homeless shelter, teach Bible studies, bring troubled teens into your home, teach tennis lessons or play doubles, complete woodworking projects, etc. What do you do together to show the light of God? You will probably end up with more than one mission in your life together. There will be a current vision, a short-term implementation, and a long-term, bucket list mission. The key is to get it put down on paper or digitally to keep you focused on what's really important.

Expect this to take more than one session to get a solid vision of it. As with everything, your mission statement will need checking into and possibly revising. Once you identify what your collective mission is, you will find many places to do ministry together as a unified couple.

Pray together about these commonalities. Ask for vision and scripture to claim and cling to when the vision seems too difficult and far away. Seek the Lord on this. Be thirsty for him to identify your "couple calling" and He will not let you stray from His path, because it glorifies His name. (*See Psalm 23:3b*) Our good Father wants us to know and live in our highest gifts.

Current Life Mission:

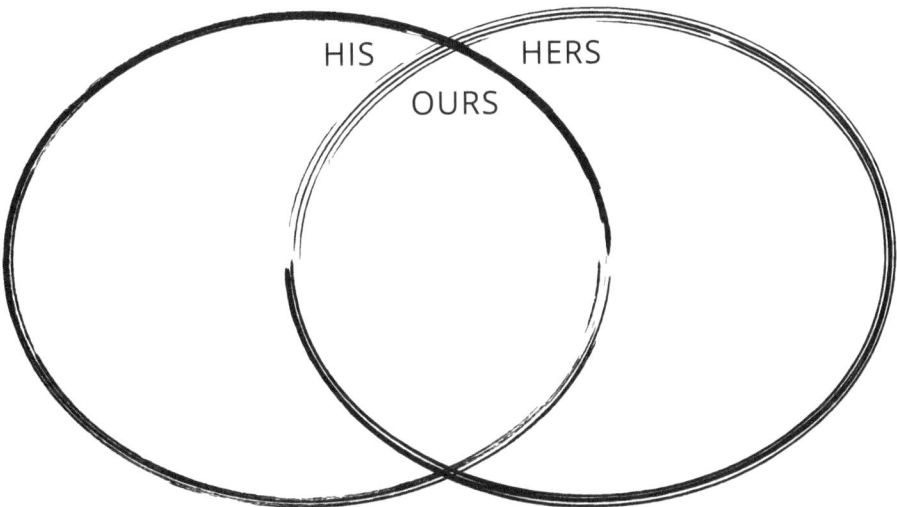

Short-Term (Upcoming Life Missions:

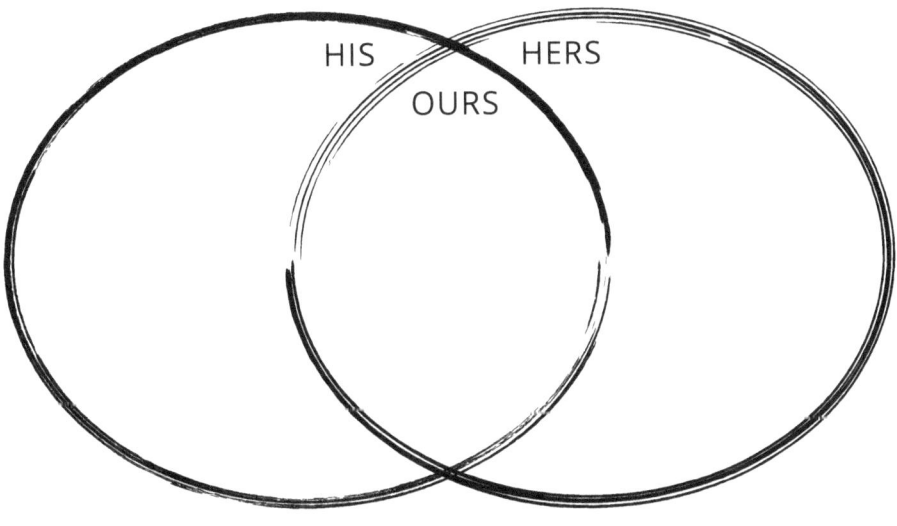

Long-term Life Missions (Bucket List):

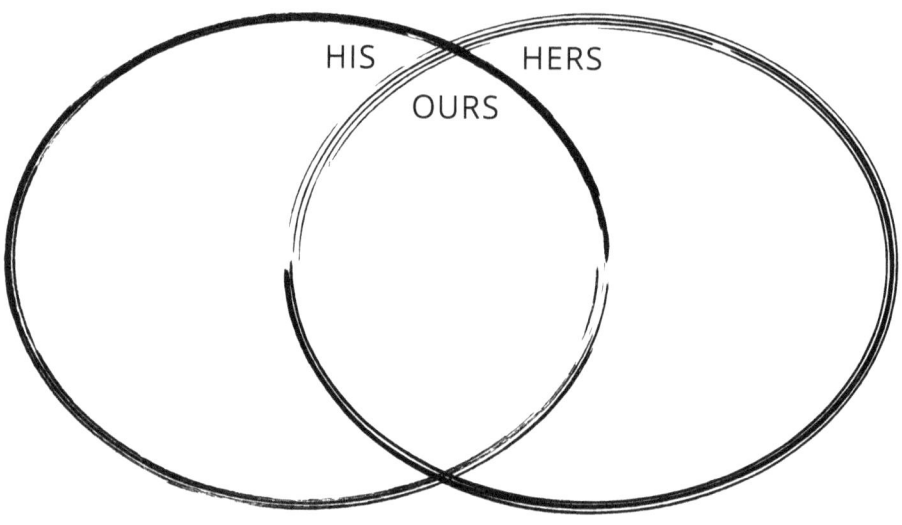

AN EXAMPLE THAT happened for Curtis and me is this: We have marriage missions written down and in business plans. We have prayed over, made plans, and identified people who are similarly called and may be a partner in our MM (marriage mission). On July 7, 2022, we received confirmation that we were operating in the correct gifting when a prophetic word was given to us while we were at a service at Grace Church Maui, our home church on the Island. We were told that I "carry a plow" and Curtis "carries a sword." We have different equipment but one calling, and we are to "teach others how to use their equipment."

I am called and better equipped at the dirty work, "getting my hands right in the turkey," while Curtis is called to "declare and decree" a less hands-on role. For a little bit of our marriage, I tried to fit Curtis into my gift. If he wasn't serving or stepping up in the manner I was, I thought he wasn't stepping up at all. Like with this book project, he is adding to the content, so you get to hear his voice as well, but the burden is on me to create the bulk of the content.

But hear me, there is no way I would be sticking my neck out in this boldness if I did not have my knight in shining armor, sword at the ready, providing protection for me all the time! Live in your individual gifts but cooperate together in your collective assignment.

Living the Honeymoon Life

I took a trip to our family farm, to get away, be alone, and do some deep work on this book. To my surprise, my family and friends were all very anxious to spend time with me. I thought I was investing in productivity, but God's purpose was about connectivity. I saw family and spent a great deal of time with my mom, Nana.

Even if I'd wanted to work, I was having extreme issues connecting to the internet and getting anything on my computer to cooperate. So, I decided not to fight it. I relaxed and cherished each moment with my loved ones.

On the final morning as I was about to leave, I prayed to the Lord. "If I am meant to get any work done here, please allow my technology to function. I turned my computer on, tethered to my phone, and found that I was connected.

Finally connecting to the internet was a rush, and I also found that I had great clarity. I was able to outline this entire season in those few precious hours, and I was so grateful.

Curtis and I had sacrificed a week together for me to get away. We had invested time and money to make sure it happened. We had prayed and planned how my trip might be a success. In the end, God had done way more than we could have planned or thought or imagined. (*See Ephesians 3:20*)

Takeaway: Don't cram my agenda onto God's blessings. Our plans are blessed when we step to the side and allow Him to guide our steps. (*See Proverbs 16:9*)

Steps to a P&A-like Marriage

- Establish your marriage mission and walk in it.
- Identify those in full-time ministry whom you can come alongside and support.
- Be a part of the solution to problems you identify in the community around you.
- Protect, to the best of your ability, the sanctity of marriage and Christianity.
- Risk! For the sake of the Gospel of Peace, put it all on the line.
- Then you will look like Priscilla and Aquila, but more than that, you will look like Jesus.

Chillax

Our children grew up in Hawaii, and it's a little harder to decipher where summer starts and stops there. There are subtle changes, but for the most part the weather is not the primary distinction. What was the sign of summer? School break. Time to "chillax," as our son coined the phrase. Summer can be a time to allow ourselves to get lost in doing little to nothing at all.

On the islands, summer meant beach time, hiking, and gathering with the Ohana—family. Our children spent long days on our rented property hunting Jackson's chameleons and eating fruit right from the trees. Summer meant childhood free time, with sleepovers and church camps thrown in.

Today, I hear a much different version: Long trips to long tournaments. Sports, band, and activities that used to end at the conclusion of the school year stretch all through the year, crowding out the simple art of boredom.

God's plan for our lives is much simpler and without the stress of constant activity. Having too many obligations crowds out the simple freedom of stopping and smelling the roses. Remember, God walked in the Garden of Eden with Adam and Eve in the "cool of the day," during a time of rest and ease.

FAITH JOURNEY

God Is Good All the Time!

Matthew 7:11: God is a perfect parent, so if we as imperfect can give good to our children, how much more should we expect from our Heavenly Father?

Psalm 118:1-2: His lovingkindness is everlasting.

1 John 5:14: He hears His children, who ask according to His will.

God, our Father in heaven, is the provider of all good things in our lives. He loves to give to His children. When we take time to get in His will, He blesses it. Remember, He loves you and cheers you on to be the best version of you!

I Will Be Better When . . .

When I was younger, and through most of my forties, I had the strangest belief system. I would think and say out loud, "I will be more organized when my kids are older." Or, "I will have more energy for the things of God when I am done with this stage of life." Or my personal favorite, "When I turn fifty, I will have it figured out." Well into my fifties, I am still waiting for the giant lightbulb to appear over my head.

But what I have learned is:

- "I will be better when I prioritize God and spend time with Him."

- "I am better when I make the best of the way things work out."

- "I can focus on what I need for the day, because God will supply all of my needs daily."

I have learned not to plan seven days' worth of activity into six days. I have learned that "no" is not a negative answer; it's a vote of confidence for what I know I must be doing. I have learned that the world will still be revolving the next day if I leave a few tasks left undone and go to bed on time.

So maybe I wasn't completely off base when I thought things would be better in the future. I just did not realize that it would come through *me* changing *me*, allowing God to be first and director of my plans. It is such a relief to see lemonade come from lemons. (One of my personal favorite summer beverages—so refreshing.)

Men, This Means You

While women are often more prone to over-commitment, men, you also can fall victim to overburdened syndrome. For example, if you have agreed to mow the lawn, and your only day to get it done is Saturday, an early-morning Saturday tee time may be off the table, at least for the season. Making first things first without compromise is learned and strengthened when there are clear boundaries in your calendar.

Making adjustments in time allotments brings peace and order to your life. Priority of God, spouse, family, work, and leisure during times of busyness cannot be misaligned. You are the spiritual leader and must lead by example.

Recipe for a Strong Marriage

Putting It All Together—Choosing Rest While Remaining Active Is an Art

To find and maintain balance during busy seasons requires thought and discipline. To maintain focus, the priorities on what is most important must be decided and agreed upon to avoid conflict.

An image I have seen played out goes like this: Your task is to fill an empty bucket with water, sand, pebbles, and rocks. Choosing the order, you do this is imperative. If you put the sand and pebbles at the bottom, the rocks will spill out over the top. If the water goes in early, the dropping of the other items can cause it to splash out and it does not allow the sand and pebbles to properly take their place. If you put the large rocks in, then pour the pebbles over them and shake them into the gaps, you maximize space. Then, sand can be added in a similar manner. At this point, the bucket may appear full, but when you slowly and carefully add the water into the mix, something miraculous happens: Everything fits within the allotted space.

The rocks are your foundation. Time with God, time as a couple, immediate family. The pebbles are church and work. The sand is community and friends. The water is all the things that you plan as enjoyment and relaxation. They all belong in the bucket. You must play. In fact, Curtis and I believe that without play it is impossible to fully live the Honeymoon Life.

The secret is the order of priority. The foundation and the most important items must be securely in place to allow everything to fit into place. A note of reality: These items will change and shift throughout your marriage, and you must be willing and open to re-evaluate and respond appropriately. Listen to God as He moves you through each season.

I am not sure how and why deviled eggs are called that except in the case of my husband, and my late father, they are too tempting to resist. They are quite basic in their ingredients and can be modified and designed to fit any occasion and holiday. In our family, deviled eggs are my assignment. The key step I will share with you is a topic of contention among foodies: how to perfectly boil eggs to ensure the peeling does not tear the whites apart. Turns out, even cooking requires laying a foundation.

Deviled Eggs

PERFECTLY BOILED EGGS: Bring 4 quarts of water in a large sauce-pan to boil. Once water is boiling, use a slotted spoon to set refrigerator-cold eggs one by one gently into the water. Boil 13 minutes. If the water stops boiling, add a minute. If it becomes a rapid boil, turn down the heat to maintain a soft boil for the 13 minutes.

Deviled Eggs

1 dozen eggs, cold	½ to ¾ cup Miracle Whip
3 small gherkin sweet pickles	2 medium dill pickles
1 Tbsp. sweet pickle juice	1 Tbsp. red onion
1 teaspoon soy sauce (shoyu)	¼ to ½ tsp. garlic powder
1 Tbsp. heaping yellow mustard	½ stalk celery
2 Tbsp. white sugar	Salt and pepper to taste

1. While eggs are boiling, finely mince celery, onion, sweet pickles, and dill pickles.

2. When the timer goes off, immediately pour off the boiling water and run sink-cold water over the eggs until water stops heating quickly. Turn water down to a slow stream. Stir eggs by hand to ensure no hot spots remain. Dump off water and add cold water and a few ice cubes. Allow to stand for 5 minutes.

3. Peel eggs using cold running water or dipping them into a pan of water. Rinse and dry each egg.

4. Cut eggs in half longways. Be careful to ensure that each egg's white remains intact.

5. In a medium mixing bowl, gently drop yolks. Place white halves onto your serving tray.

6. Using a fork, or potato masher, crumble yolks into fine pieces.

7. Add garlic powder, a little salt and pepper; stir. Add veggies and pickles; stir. Add wet ingredients and mix until smooth, then taste to ensure desired flavor has been reached. Additional salt and pepper can really bring out all the flavors at this point.

8. Note: Think about when you fill the whites. Once the mix sits, it will bring more flavor out. However, once the whites are filled, the flavor is tamed by the whites.

9. Using a spoon or melon baller, scoop mix into each egg white half.

10. Sprinkle lightly with paprika for garnish if desired. Refrigerate until ready to serve. I don't like to put the eggs in the refrigerator for more than 2 hours, so I balance all of my other cooking duties with the timing of the deviled eggs. If cooking space is an issue, eggs can be boiled several hours before and peeled and left in cool water. Dry thoroughly before beginning the assembly process.

Growth Requires Energy

In nature, summer is the time for growing fruit. Plants expend their energy to grow themselves and bring fruit to fullness. All the while, animals are growing and caring for their offspring and eating as much of the provision as possible. Summer is hectic.

Families with school-age children often plan vacations and attend endless sporting activities and vacation Bible school events. There may be sleepovers and campouts in the backyard, utilizing every moment of light, which can last 15 hours a day in peak summer.

Professionally, summers encompass long work hours to climb the ladder. It might include continuing education while working full-time, then once the promotions are realized the added responsibility comes with longer hours.

Families in childbearing years are busy chasing toddlers, changing diapers, and attending play dates. Mothers who stayed home while raising children may decide to start a career or go back to school.

We also have volunteer and social activities, plus hobbies and chores around the house. Some of us are just naturally inclined to say yes too often and keep a full agenda at all times, leaving little to no margin for God to call us anywhere. How can we, in this rat-race society, find balance and stillness in the fast-paced world?

CURTIS' INPUT

Balancing Act

After a lot of prayers and tearful eyes, we moved from our home in Sigourney, Iowa, to Oahu in July 2003. We lived in a small three-bedroom apartment in Salt Lake, an area in Honolulu, (aka, the Concrete Jungle). I was working for STI, a small research and development company. The work was interesting, and the people were genuinely enthusiastic about what we were accomplishing. Less than a year later, BAE, a huge defense contractor, bought us out. Their education benefits were amazing, so Terri and I agreed that I should return to school to get my bachelor's degree; I had earned an AS in 1992. I wanted to get my degree quickly but didn't know how much extra load I could handle. The school I chose offered accelerated courses, so this could really help with finishing more quickly. If I took one or two three- to four-credit courses at a time, it would still take nearly three years to complete. We decided to speed that up. This took another all-in approach; Terri would understand what this would require more than I did. I started off by ploughing ahead: working, eating dinner when I got home, and then hopping into studies until our normal bedtime. *SCREECH!!!*

Not too much time went by when Terri sat me down and said, "Honey, I appreciate all the hard work you are putting in for work and school. I know we want to get ahead. But you need to carve out time for your kids—and me." As the tunnel-vision guy I was, this was a shock. I knew she was right, but it had just skipped my mind. DOH! I made a suggested schedule, which was completely reasonable to me. Okay, I can stay up an extra hour I suppose. . . I am sure Terri was trying to patiently listen about my lame schedule.

Two hours for my family, while I was spending fourteen hours going to work or school, was not acceptable. Terri spelled it out for me as I really needed it then: When I get home at 5:30–6:00, I needed to spend from then until 9:00 as family time, with emphasis on the kids. Then, 9:00 to 10:00 would be Terri time. Schoolwork would be after that. . . Weekends, on the other hand, were when we loved taking time to enjoy the wonderful island God had planted us on. Typically, we would go to the beach on Saturday and then Sunday after church just about every weekend. Once classes started, though, Terri would take the kids both days to the beach and I would plan to hit the beach one of those days. When tests came, though, there was no fun beach time for ol' Curt.

There was no way this was going to work for the next two-plus years. How could I possibly do schoolwork every night until one or two in the morning? Not going to happen. Terri told me to figure it out—not in a mean way, just matter-of-factly. Then I remembered something my brother, Gene, had told me when he was in a similar situation years before: "Curt, you can do this too. You go without sleep, you power through it, because the end goal is worth it." When he said this to me it was 11 p.m. I was on vacation, just hanging with him at his house. I was hitting the sack, and he was just hitting the books. Living on three to four hours of sleep a night isn't fun, but it is do-able—for a season.

This balancing act lasted for twenty-two months. Yes, we sped it up that much. Perhaps we had to slack somewhere? The kids felt left out? My grades definitely had to suffer, right? Friction between Terri and Me? The truth is none of the above. Terri managed all of the family details, while I concentrated the majority of my efforts on work and school. I have never done so well academically. We were living in one of America's most expensive economies on one small income, spending great family time at some of the world's best beaches, turning my optical alignment passion into a real career, and demonstrating to our children how much can be accomplished with very little.

You and your spouse can do it too! Those obstacles in your way are there to make you better. To stretch your limits. To reach your greatest dreams and potential.

Study on Busyness or Making Children the Center of Marriage

WHILE JESUS MINISTERED on earth, He called twelve men to be His inner circle. He poured out His life for them and disregarded His own needs and comforts to ensure they were being prepared to carry the Church forward after His crucifixion. But they were not the center of His world while on earth. They were His responsibility and His closest companions, but God the Father was His utmost focus. The will of the Father and staying connected to His Father through prayer and fasting was Jesus' first priority. His disciples, like our children, are to be treated as very important and held in high regard, but children or career or even Church volunteer obligations cannot dominate our focus, time, and energy.

Like Jesus, God the Father, and our walk with Jesus, allowing the Holy Spirit to guide us is our number one calling. After that, our spouse, our one flesh, our union, must be next. If we show division and unbalance within our marriage, our children will pick up on that. It can cause them to fear, or they may attempt to drive a further wedge to get the center spot of the household attention.

An article from the Marriage Dynamics Institute website[7] cites the very real crisis that child-centered marriages have brought to our culture. Divorce rates among couples in their fifties and sixties have "more than doubled since 1990." There is also the psychological damage done by helicopter parenting, leaving those children anxious and unable to cope well into adulthood. The helicopter parenting and over-commitment to children's activities, while neglecting the marriage, turns out to be neither good for the marriage nor the children.

The priority list we, as Honeymoon Lifers, must maintain is God first, spouse second, kids third, work (both at home and professionally) fourth, then outside activities. I would include overcommitment to church volunteering in the last category; there is a difference between answering our calling and saying yes to everything. You should account for corporate worship and fellowship within your calendar, but there must be independent time in the Word and prayer as well. Growing only in public can lead to shallow roots. (*See Matthew 13: 20-21*)

Living the Honeymoon Life

It is impossible to be the example of Christ to the world without having balance and a shared vision within your marriage. As Christ led His disciples with a servant leader's heart, so must we be considerate and compassionate to our spouse's schedule and time. Remember, time is our only non-renewable resource.

Communication is a big part of creating a culture of mutually satisfying relationships. We do not advocate that you sugarcoat or manipulate your spouse, but rather consider the person on the other end of the request. Keeping your eye on the endgame is huge when chores must be done, bills must be paid, and children's needs must be met. But your life is more than the accomplishments of these tasks.

In the area of household tasks, Curtis and I use "win-win language" whenever possible. For example, if there is something I need his help with (or for him to just do; I am basically worthless when it comes to plumbing, except to run for an occasional tool), I think about how I should ask him. When I have a need that can wait, I start my request with: "It does not have to be right now, but I would really appreciate it if you could fix the toilet in the master bath that is leaking." Or if something is time sensitive, I may say instead, "If you could make time within the next twenty-four hours to fix the toilet in the master bath, please do so because the leaking has gotten pretty severe." These requests give the partner the timeframe and an insight into how bad the need is. Setting our spouses up to succeed in what we are asking from them saves a lot of disappointment down the road and helps everyone have their needs met.

Fresh Starts and Do-Overs

When It Comes to Family

SUMMER OFTEN MARKS a time of family reunions and gatherings. The word *honeymoon* is derived from June moon, a time when most weddings traditionally take place. But when it comes to family. . . even Jesus struggled.

The Bible records Jesus' mother and brothers coming to him, during the height of His ministry, assumedly to talk some sense into Him. (*See Matthew 12:47-50*) He saw conflict among his first followers even though there were only a dozen. (*See Luke 9:46*) So, if the perfect Son of Man struggled with human relationships, it should be expected we will as well.

Messy, complicated, and difficult relationships do not give us license to slink into a hole and live a solitary life. Jesus modeled sacrificial love when he wept over Jerusalem. (*See Luke 19:41*) Like many of the prophets, Jesus knew that the people he came to save with his life-giving message and ultimate sacrifice would turn their backs on him.

How can I apply Jesus' example of servant love? By staying in the battle.

Last year we had a family reunion at our family farm. People from all over the USA, including Hawaii, flew in or drove RVs or cars to attend. It was beautifully orchestrated and planned, thanks to my daughter Victoria and niece Markie. But there was drama, and plenty of it. Some came in blow-ups, some in passive-aggressive moves, some refusing to be in the same company with another person. . . In the end, however, people reconnected with family. We were reminded why we enjoy each other and just celebrated our common heritage. I reconnected with cousins I had not spoken to in decades. I even visited family in Florida who could not make the trip.

Was it stressful? Yes!

Was it worth it? DEFINITELY! Or to quote the commercial: "Priceless!"

Consider it all joy, my brothers and sisters,
when you encounter various trials.

JAMES 1:2

SALT AND LIGHT

Finding Your North

As Christians united in holy matrimony, there is only one place to set our compass true. The Word of God is the final authority on what we hear, see, or think we know. If the sermon does not line up with scripture, it is not to be allowed to sink in and become a guide to our feet. If our friend's advice does not meet scriptural integrity, it is not a light unto our path. Even our own interpretations or desires can lead us astray. By prayerfully reading scripture, while allowing the Holy Spirit to be our filter, we can rest assured that we are aligned with truth.

Then it is our commission to carry truth to all the earth. That is the reason you are holding this book. God said "write," so I started writing. Along the way I met the people who could assist me in getting the book out to those whom God intends to have it serve. And I am praying for each of you as you read it.

All Scripture is inspired by God and beneficial for teaching,
for rebuke, for correction, for training in righteousness.

2 TIMOTHY 3:16

 FUN & GAMES

Wake Up and Smell the Coffee

Most of our busy season hours are already spoken for, so making time to be together as a couple can be a challenge. Finding moments to steal away as Jesus modeled in His life here on earth can safeguard our balance.

For Curtis and me, vacation in Maui is a very hectic and scheduled event. We love it, but we have learned through the years to schedule times that we are alone and not allow anything to interfere. We generally have the grandkids staying with us in the condo, so a quiet morning devotional with a delicious cup of Maui coffee is the ideal start to our busy day. Now that they are older, we can take our coffee across the street to the beach even when they are with us. They like the slow start to the day as well, playing video games or watching shows and snacking on Costco muffins.

While you may be on a staycation at home or enjoying a quick getaway across town, the same strategy can be used to make time together. Weekend mornings can be the ideal time to just soak up each other's attention. A slow roll out of bed, a devotional time in some new location, and a favorite morning treat make the rest of the demanding day seem less daunting. Moments that refresh and balance act as nourishment for your soul.

SUMMER

Krupp Marriage Experience

*Things Work Out Best for Those Who Make
the Best of the Way Things Work Out.*

—KIM

CURTIS AND I have been in many circumstances that left us feeling stranded. On one flight back to the mainland from Hawaii with our four children, we unwittingly booked a layover in Santa Cruz, California, with an early morning extended layover. Six hours to be exact. Santa Cruz, being a smaller airport, does not have services in the middle of the night. We were even moved out of the terminal. We found a spot in the check-in area out of the way, and near some vending machines.

Fortunately, I had the kids each pack a small blanket and a stuffed animal in their carry-ons. Toothbrushes and snacks were in their backpacks. Somehow, we made a little circle that was quite comfortable. We had a couple of cell phones at the time, a couple of DS game consoles, and a laptop. There were enough outlets to plug in whatever was running out of battery. We snacked and watched movies and played cards and other games we brought. The kids got extra screen time and each of us napped at some point.

Our son, about four years old at the time, commented, "We are living like hobos!" He was very excited about it. While we were careful never to repeat this itinerary, it remains a great story in our family legacy: the night we lived like hobos.

Not every honeymoon story I hear is negative, but many have reports of growing and shaping the newlyweds in directions they did not anticipate. Family vacations and reunions bring an entirely new level and opportunity for plans to go wrong. When the luggage is lost, the flight is canceled, or the purse is stolen, how can we recover what was meant to be joyful and restful?

You've heard the phrase "If life gives you lemons, make lemonade." Well, make your lemonade. In this technology-ladened world it is easier than ever to cancel credit cards and book new travel plans. While waiting for the solution, take time to adjust the agenda to meet the new schedule. Allow creativity to show you more options than you thought about prior to the misfortune. The important thing is that we rarely pack up and go home when things do not go our way while traveling. Bring that fight attitude into everything you and your spouse face.

Leap Day to Reset Our Calendars— Sabbatical to Reset Our Hearts

Leap Day! What a great concept! The full yearly rotation of the earth is approximately 365.25 days. If the quarter of the day were ignored long-term, our calendar seasons would be thrown out of whack. Our lives and mindsets are much like the calendar. Despite incremental warnings and nudging from our internal calendars, we often fail to make adjustments to realign our minds, bodies, and hearts.

Not long ago, I owned a franchise lawn maintenance company. I really enjoyed the work and the people, but the stress it was putting on me mentally and physically was becoming undeniable. I was gaining weight and had trouble sleeping. I talked at warp speed, sometimes neglecting to complete one thought before starting another. Curtis and I would spend late nights working on equipment and long weekends catching up on services, all while he worked his full-time job. All the signs were there; I was slowly trading my health for the success of my business. After much prayer and distress, we decided to put the business on the market. Within a year, it sold, and I began the slow process of de-stressing my life and getting my health back.

Our marriages likewise need and deserve a reset. For Curtis and me, learning to relax and settle back into a more balanced life has not been automatic, but just by being intentional about it we are starting to see progress.

Through the process of learning how to adjust my habits and become much better balanced, I noticed that I was in much worse condition than I even realized. I started to notice that my heart raced occasionally, and I had some symptoms of high blood pressure. The weight gain was just the tip of the iceberg. It was not until I slowed down and hit reset that I was able to see and hear all that was happening right inside my own body and mind.

Course correction requires constant attention. Consider this: If you are traveling by plane and off course by just one degree over a short distance, from Dallas to Houston, you end up 4.3 miles off course. It's walkable, and you are at least still in Texas. But over longer treks without course correction the results become exponential. Flying from Dallas to London, off by one degree without any course correction you would end up 83 miles off course, putting you somewhere in the English Channel.

This example doesn't even factor in changing wind direction and currents. We might be tempted during the busy season to ignore recalibration and course correction, but if we do, we can find ourselves quite lost later in life.

Perhaps, like me, you need to slow down and take a leap day. Perhaps dedicate a month to resetting habits and hopes and relationships. Just like a calendar, with even a slight deviation over a long enough time, we can end up way off course.

And do not be conformed to this world, but be transformed by the renewing of your mind, so that you may prove what the will of God is—that which is good, and acceptable and perfect.

ROMANS 12:2

Reinforce Memory Verse

Our memory verse reminds us to listen for Jesus to call us out of the busyness—to step away, even when it seems like the world will stop revolving if we take some downtime. We can tend to have a superhero complex, thinking our calling is to save the world. But the truth is that Jesus worked the majority of His ministry in small groups: gathered with His disciples, at dinner parties, personal invitations to homes, visiting friends and family, going to houses. . . Of course, He taught at the synagogue and to large crowds, but the focus was always personal touch. His love for the masses did not drive Him to perform fly-by healings and mass miracles. He interacted with those in His path and taught His disciples to do the same.

When the time for rest was required, Jesus commanded them to "come away."

Take out your calendar, or open it on the phone, and look for an opening within the next fourteen days to get away. If you can afford an overnight, book that. If you can afford a day's drive, book that. If childcare is an issue, consider taking a date day while the kids are in school.

We love to look up destinations within two hours and find out what there is to do and eat there. Find local hotspots and learn a few names. A two-hour drive, especially on backroads, gives you space and time to get in deep, uninterrupted conversations. The idea is to get out of the routine of the day and take long, deep breaths of fresh, new air.

Jesus in the Wilderness for Forty Days

Jesus fasted and prayed in the wilderness in preparation for His public ministry. (*See Luke 4:1-21 and Matthew 4:1-11*) The scriptures tell us that after He became hungry, the Devil tempted Him. The first temptation was to satisfy His physical hunger: making bread from stones; meeting His own needs through His divine power. He was tempted to use His divine nature on earth and take His place as earthly ruler. Satan even attempted to have Jesus "test God" by throwing Himself down. Jesus did not succumb to any of these suggestions, but each time He responded by quoting scripture and correcting the devil's use of God's word.

While we won't fast for 40 days without eating or drinking, there is great value in getting off the beaten path and allowing our weaknesses to be revealed to us through the Spirit. Jesus would later face all of these issues again in His ministry. This time away alone, after the Holy Spirit had settled on Him, was proof that He was ready.

I believe we are given a glimpse of these temptations to help us realize that being tempted by something is not the sin; humoring it and giving into it is. Jesus set the clear example. At first sight of temptation, call it out and walk the other way.

In the heat of the summer, while life is demanding all of our energy and faculties, we must commit to and practice resisting temptation.

Ronnie's Potato Salad

THE RECIPES CONTAINED in the handwritten cookbook from my mother-in-law inspire my husband to relive childhood memories and help me learn about how he came to be who he is.

Potato Salad

10 potatoes, cooked & diced
1 Green pepper, chopped
4 Sweet pickles "
4 Dill pickles "
5 radishes, cut & diced
2 stalks of celery - chopped
1 cucumber, chopped

Ronnie Krupp

½ onion chopped
2 tb. mustard
½ cup miracle whip

. Mix all together in bowl. Add miracle whip and mustard mix well. Put in refrigerator over night for best taste.

Several years before my wonderful mother-in-law passed away, my sister-in-law, Jill, helped her put several of her family favorite recipes together in a cookbook for us all. It is a treasure that I keep handy and use on occasion. This Polish potato salad is something Curtis has mastered. I love when my husband cooks.

One of the secrets of this potato salad (that is not revealed here) is that Ronnie (my mother-in-law) boiled the potatoes with the skins on, then cooled and peeled them afterward. It was very common back in her generation to keep just a small piece of information to yourself so that you would always be known as, for example, the "Queen of Polish Potato Salad" and no one could replicate it exactly.

Coming Away Takes Many Forms

Curtis and I have learned to find the quiet in just about every way. Learning to tithe quiet time into our relationship, especially during busy seasons, cements a habit that will linger all of our lives.

- **Daily**: morning devotionals with coffee. He gets up about 4:30 a.m. (I didn't know that 4:30 came twice a day!), so I wake up, do devotionals, then go back to sleep.

- **Weekly**: We Sabbath from Saturday evening to Sunday evening. We attend church, sit on the loveseat (if you don't have one, I highly recommend the investment; best snuggle spot!), lay in our bed, nap, kayak, play with our grandson, eat leftovers, etc. We also have weekly dates. These can be a quiet dinner for just the two of us, out or in. We will drive to somewhere new or a favorite spot, enjoy a sit-down at our local cigar lounge, or engage in another activity.

- **Monthly**: We take a weekend getaway or staycation each month. We use this time to check in on our vision, mission, finances, mental health, physical satisfaction (yes, we ask how we are meeting each other's sexual desires), and spiritual state. These little investments over a night or two have proven to be worth every penny and moment invested.

- **Annually**: We are so richly blessed to get away to Maui each year. There have been a few exceptions, but generally it is a three-week respite. It takes that long to fit in all the family, church, and friends. We want to stay invested in those precious relationships.

These are our commitments. They meet our love languages and budget of time and money, and they keep us intimately connected to God and each other. Find your rhythm of "coming away" that fills your life with joy and rest.

Summer May Go Quickly; Autumn Is Just Around the Corner

No matter how well you plan and maintain, you will at some point find yourself in Autumn. For Curtis and me, we don't plan to "retire" in the traditional sense. We want to continue to be in the field of usefulness until we are called home to glory. Autumn does not mean being put out to pasture. We believe that reward is eternal. No, our later days are meant to reap the harvest of all that we have sown throughout our lives, and to share with the younger generation how to make their own Honeymoon Life.

Happy Honeymooning!

AUTUMN

BALD EAGLES

Bald eagles have a courtship ritual that is both fascinating and dangerous, known as the "death spiral." (Has your marriage ever felt like that? Ours has!) They lock talons midair and then free-fall until they are just above the ground. This dangerous practice does occasionally end in death for both eagles, if they delay in letting go too long. The courtship practice does have practical purposes, one being ensuring the mates are compatible and strong enough for the monogamous lifelong mating they are about to enter.

THE BALD EAGLE is our national bird, a symbol of strength, freedom, and wisdom. Notice that it is the mature eagle that we have as our icon, not a juvenile. An eagle must be mature to master all that it must learn to become mating- and hunting-ready, making this fierce predator the apex standard of relationship building.

Reaping What We Have Sown and Finding Joy in Our New Roles

Throughout all the other seasons of life, we tend to be geared to saving for a rainy day. Autumn is a time of reaping what has been sown. Often our children start to visit our homes to celebrate holidays, or if we prefer, we put them in charge of the celebrations and visit theirs. Our work may be winding down or we may have moved out of a full-time professional career. But this season of our marriage should never be viewed as retired or out to pasture.

The energy and bustle of all of the other seasons of life should be relished and enjoyed in our Autumn season, just at a pace more consistent with contentment and ease. God never intends for us to believe and live as if we have outlived our usefulness or purpose in life. If you or your marriage seems to be lingering in things of the past, it is time to evaluate what you have accomplished and how you can leverage those experiences for the benefit of the future.

While there may be evidence of the years on our skin, there must be evidence of the experiences and wisdom that have etched themselves indelibly in the better people and union we have become. Don't allow the sirens of regret or fear to steal the joy out of this wonderful season of your life and marriage. God still needs you on the field. You still have a role to play!

Anyone who thinks fallen leaves
are dead has never watched them
dancing on a windy day.

SHIRA TAMIR

AUTUMN

The Season

So Easy, a Caveman Could Do It—NOT!

I must admit, I didn't know what marriage really entailed when we got married almost thirty-five years ago. I was very self-absorbed and not thoughtful—at all. I had to learn how to think of others and maybe not be so concerned about my comfort. Terri is the most thoughtful person I know. She even thinks about those people who knock on our door selling something. She buys from every kid who knocks on the door, while I was the opposite.

What happens over thirty-five years with someone you love deeply is that you not only try to be a blessing to them, but you take on some of their traits. Through osmosis, I have learned to be more thoughtful and actually care more for people because of my life with Terri.

The person (usually us men) who says "I won't change for anyone" is either fooling himself or dragging his knuckles. No offense to cavemen here. So, the wife you fought to marry isn't worth your time trying to continue to impress and love?

More and more I find myself trying to show the bride of my youth that I still desire her and even surprise her with that deed or gift she wasn't expecting.

Scripture to Memorize Together

Therefore, we do not lose heart, but though our outer person is decaying, yet our inner person is being renewed day by day.

2 CORINTHIANS 4:16

I LOVE AUTUMN, or "fall" as we like to refer to it, due to the deciduous trees losing their leaves. It is a beautiful and crisp season, with perfect temperatures for walks in nature and enjoying the changing colors of the trees. It is a time of bountiful harvest and storage of excess produce from the summer's growth. This gentle connector between summer and winter offers so much opportunity if we are wise enough to look at the positive.

Natural to Experience: Autumn May Cause Us to Reflect on What Our Lives Have Meant

While visiting Pittsburgh, Pennsylvania, I toured the Heinz Museum. I highly recommend taking the time to go if you are ever in the area.

I enjoyed learning about the sports and technology advancements that came from the area. I had no idea that Lewis started his famous expedition here and met up with Clark later. I learned how glass and steel have been improved and enhanced in this area. The Pittsburgh area offers a host of contributions to the world. The Carnegie empire originated here, as did the first organ transplants. The Pittsburgh area is home to Fred Rogers and Andy Warhol, and it was an important hub of the underground railroad.

I stood at a display of a young prairie girl tending to the cooking. On the small table next to her was a handwritten book. The plaque in front of the display informed me that it was a cookbook, complete with ingredients and amounts and directions for cooking. This young girl's mom or aunt had created a cookbook to ensure that family favorites could be served for generations to come—a "novel" concept at the time.

At first, I thought, *Wow, how progressive to have the forethought in that difficult life of taming the prairie to make the effort to create a cookbook!* Then it occurred to me that the woman might not have been much more noble or altruistic than I am. She was probably responding to necessity, repeatedly instructing the same dishes over and over each time they were made.

It isn't always the noble ideas that cause the progress to be realized; sometimes, it's the simple reality that *my life will be better if I bother to do this.* But as I walked through the museum it occurred to me that these people are famous now, but in their day they all struggled with self-doubt and confidence. Like them, it is the responsibility of all of us to live our lives to positively impact the future. It is within each human being to play their role so that those who come after us are better off.

It is common in the Autumn of our lives to consider what our lives will mean to future generations if we make a difference. It makes me ask myself a few questions: Beyond taking care of what I need, what will my contribution to this world be? What lasting effect will our marriages have on the world around us? If we just walk the path God has laid out for us, our lives will have eternal impact. Remember, on the third day after Jesus' crucifixion, Mary and the ladies were just going through the ritual that was the custom for them to perform. The act of performing their civic duty in obedience put them in position to be first to encounter the risen Jesus.

Now after the Sabbath, as it began to dawn toward
the first *day* of the week, Mary Magdalene and
the other Mary came to look at the tomb.

MATTHEW 28:1

Counting It All Joy!

While Autumn can be a time when people get comfortable and settle down, we decided instead to go exploring. For Curtis and me, this habit has kept our romance alive. (Well, that and keeping the physical intimacy exciting!) An adventure we chose when we could have slowed down was to buy a franchise.

I had been substitute-teaching through the child-raising years of our family to keep the same schedule as the children. So, when the time was right, I got my teaching certificate and began teaching full-time. After a few years in the classroom and putting up with the challenges in the educational climate, I decided it just wasn't where I wanted to be. I took an online gig for ESL (English as a Second Language) through a company teaching Chinese children English. I loved it! It was good money, and it was easy to build relationships with the students. But the hours were terrible. Classes started at 3:30 a.m., not my golden hour.

One morning after finishing ten classes back-to-back (thirty minutes each for a five-hour day), I received an email that normally you would find in spam. "We found your resume on Indeed and think you would be well-suited for business ownership. Take this brief survey." Instead of sending it to the trash, I took the survey. As soon as I hit "send," I called Curtis and said, "I think I just got us into something. Buckle up!"

Within minutes I got a response, and we started our journey toward franchise ownership. We worked with a franchise coach and did "due diligence," researching three different models. (Not all franchises are created equal!) After six months, we had made a decision and our journey in this new reality took off.

Here's the romantic part. At the time we started this journey, our home life was a mess. Three of our four children were still at home, and they were rebelling in every way. From the surface, this was the absolute worst time to consider starting a business. But God is faithful.

Over the next five and a half years, we built a business and met some of the finest people on earth. The other franchise owners became our friends and mentors. Through networking, I met some of my closest friends –other business owners. During this period, one of our children was facing a felony charge. God laid it on my heart that I needed twelve women praying for me. Of the twelve God brought into my heart, only four were church-connected friends. The other eight were strong businesswomen who lived out their faith in the marketplace. It turns out it was the community I needed "for such a time as this." (*See Esther 4:14*)

While the struggle was painful during these difficult times, God gave me a community that was ready to walk with me in the struggle. I can say without a doubt that despite the difficulty of business ownership, that franchise saved our lives in many ways, including giving me something outside of everyday difficulties to be the focus of my attention. The community we built in that time includes some of our strongest relationships. In the end, I can be truly thankful for the struggles and trials because what it awarded me was of far greater value than what it cost.

There is an old TV series, *Cheers*, that exemplifies what the Church should look like. The show revolves around a local bar called Cheers. The regulars in the bar truly make a community. The theme song says it best: "Sometimes you want to go where everybody knows your name." Church, take note: Everybody wants to go where they are welcomed and called by name. Like the first-century church, we must live daily in community with our faith family, not just on Sunday in corporate worship.

That's where we need to "up our game" as followers of Jesus. We and our church family need to get outside of the walls of the building and take it to the streets. We need to do marketplace ministry. The goal is not to take time off work to do ministry, but to make our workplace our ministry. If every Christian got up every morning giving God control of every aspect of their day, it would change the world and put the news media out of business.

The day we find the perfect church, it becomes imperfect the moment we join it.

CHARLES H. SPURGEON

CURTIS' INPUT

My Adrenaline Rush

Terri always has had an entrepreneurial spirit. She has ingrained it into our children, thankfully. I, on the other hand, do not have that same desire. So, when Terri asked if I would go into business with her, I said, "As long as you are running it, I am in!"

Helping run a business and working full-time was challenging. But it also was exhilarating. Grabbing something quick to eat after working all day, and then working until 11:00 to 12:00 at night, usually on equipment, was addicting to me. I miss it, really, but at the same time I am grateful for not having my foot on the gas pedal constantly.

The season that Terri and I spent building our Lawn Doctor franchise was an experience I would not have missed. We grew closer to each other and stretched our personal and professional limits. The other franchisees were amazing people to learn from. They were always available to help, even late at night.

It was interesting: Although I had less time to sleep, I was still excited to get up and go to work the next morning. I guess it was a nonstop adrenaline rush. Life with my Crazy Girl can be just that: crazy.

Love Your Spouse—The Danger of Slowing Down

LET'S GET REAL: When we hear the expression "we just fell out of love," or "I'm not in love with my spouse anymore," it is spoken out of a place of laziness. I don't sugarcoat these things.

It's a sad reality that love has been misrepresented even in our Christian marriages. We treat love as a feeling, when love requires action. When we live out our love between each other, practicing the attributes of love, we ensure that we cannot wake up one day "out of love" with someone.

According to the Bible, "Love is patient, love is kind, it is not jealous; love does not brag, it is not arrogant. It does not act disgracefully, it does not seek its own *benefit*; it is not provoked, does not keep an account of a wrong *suffered*, it does not rejoice in unrighteousness, but rejoices with the truth; it keeps every confidence, it believes all things, hopes all things, endures all things. Love never fails." (*1 Corinthians 13:4-8a*)

When someone says they fell "out of love," they are really saying, "I stopped being kind, patient, and trustworthy with my spouse." When we choose to love, we automatically are bound by the character traits that go along with love.

If you struggle to act in love, start with just one of love's habits and build from there. For example, keep no records of wrongs. Can you name the exact day and hour that your spouse goofed it up royally? Do you say things like "He always forgets our anniversary until I remind him!" or "She always plans a family gathering on my tee time!" Those are records of wrongs. Loving our spouses means letting go of the things in our minds and hearts that record their shortcomings. Love doesn't mean we ignore habits of neglect or abuse; we must address issues we are having. A foundation of love means we work together on building a strong love habit.

Exercising love requires effort. A mechanism Curtis uses to ensure he does not neglect certain love practices is to set a calendar reminder on his phone. My personal favorite is the alarm at 11:45

a.m. that says, "Pray for Terri." That is love in action! And like every muscle, if we exercise it, it gets stronger.

Love Notes—Wired to Love Deeply

Can you remember a time when, just when you needed something, it came through? Like you didn't know if you would make it to payday and you find $20. Some little gesture that says, "Hey, I got you!" Many times for me it has been a meaningful song, an unexpected call from a friend, a blessing that I could not have imagined. When these moments have happened to you, have you stopped and thanked God for these "love notes"? Some people would argue they are coincidence, but I know better. Just take a little time and look up at the night sky or spend time in the mountains or at the ocean. There is no denying that your Heavenly Father, who created all things, is also the Author of Romance. He loves you!

It stands to reason, then, that if we are created in His image, we too would be romantic like our Father. The deep passion that we share to our spouse is practice for our eternal life with God the Father in heaven. Knowing and being fully known or loved is a fundamental human desire. Curtis is the king of love notes. He writes them on Post-It notes or scraps of paper and leaves them somewhere for me to find later. Somehow, they are always discovered just when I need them the most. He hand-makes my occasions cards as well, drawing pictures of the scenes we love to play, like us at the beach. Back when the kids were little, he wrote letters with lots of little illustrations for them. We have saved all of these beautiful tokens of his affection for us. When you take the time to consider how others receive your gifts, you get really good at delivering them.

On the contrary, our culture tries so hard to convince us that sexually promiscuous people are living the best life. It is just not true; science catches up with the Word of God every time.

The evidence is that couples in a monogamous marriage who are Christians report the most satisfaction in their relationships. The highest satisfaction is reported by Christian married women in monogamous committed relationships.[8] Ladies! God's design is not to deny us but to keep us safely within the boundaries of the deepest, most satisfying, and most fulfilling union.

We have proved in our marriage that the closer and more intimately we walk with God, attempting to live like Jesus and allowing the Holy Spirit to influence us, the more vulnerable we can be with each other. Which, of course, is a foundational element to true intimacy.

Who Am I in Christ?

God Does Not Put Us Out to Pasture

AUTUMN IN OUR lives and marriages can be viewed negatively, as if the best of our lives is behind us. A "midlife crisis" can cause someone to do things out of character and to the extreme. Reliving the glory days of our youth rarely causes us to feel better about our aging condition. We should choose to look at Autumn as the season of reaping what we have worked so hard for all of our lives. We should be excited for the opportunity to reap a harvest of all that we have worked for throughout the other seasons in our lives. It is a time to continue learning and to pass along that which we have learned—perhaps doing better with our grandchildren then we feel we did with our children.

For Curtis and me, this season has been the most joyful and has proven to us that we still have a lot to learn about life and each other. God continues to put opportunities in our path. We must see Autumn in its true light; the time to put up some of our harvest but also to share the bounty of what we have produced.

And even to old age and gray, God, do not
abandon me, until I declare Your strength to this
generation, your power to all who are to come.

PSALM 71:18

TRUE NORTH

God Is Not Finished with You

TAKE SOME TIME to consider all that God has done for you so far. Perhaps you look through old photo albums of your younger days together. Reminisce about the good times and blessings. Give testimony to the difficult things God has already brought you through.

Now: Considering all the skills, talents, and experiences you have built along the way, identify what God is calling you to in the future? Perhaps you have time and money to invest in your grandchildren or in travel that has been put on hold. Perhaps you can answer the call to take an international mission trip. Perhaps you are called to start a ministry or write a book. You may be investing time with an aging parent. If you don't yet know what is coming next, relax in the knowledge that God still has great plans for you. You are not done until He calls you home.

> For I am confident of this very thing, that He who began a good work among you will complete it by the day of Christ Jesus.
>
> **PHILIPPIANS 1:6**

Your Marriage in Autumn

FOR A MARRIAGE, this time of slowing down can be difficult. The risk is to only look back at all the glory days and neglect the value of all that you have accomplished in the past, which makes you more fit for what God has next. This has led to an epidemic in our culture called "Silver Splitters" or "Gray Divorce." How foolish that we neglect the wisdom and knowledge we have gained, all the growth we have realized, and throw it all away. Our rich history together is to be used for good and is a great commodity in our world.

It is heartbreaking to think of these long-term relationships dissolving, and even more when we read many of the reasons that are cited[9]:

1. Grown apart: empty nest or retirement

2. Intimacy

3. Self-improvement and differing energy level gaps

4. Money/spending habits

5. Longer life expectancy.

These late-term divorces have made their way into the Church just as strongly as the rest of our society. We have done a very poor job within the Church of raising the marriage to the value that God has designed it to be. We must treat our marriages with the same kind of care and attention that we show our most valuable possessions.

Consider your marriage to be like a classic muscle car. (Ours is a 1964.5 Mustang, and trust me, there is constant maintenance on that thing.) But, unlike newer models, you are investing in an asset that continues growing in value instead of depreciating. To keep the marriage purring like a well-oiled machine, you must do maintenance along the way. The more mileage you put on your vehicle, your marriage, the more intense and more demanding the maintenance schedule becomes. Your marriage is a collector's piece; treat it with that level of respect!

Here's a test: Consider the last time you and your spouse were alone. What did you do? Did you have a meaningful connection and conversation? When was the last time you paused for a long, passionate kiss? The more attention you give to anything, the healthier it gets. Your marriage must be a credit in your life, not a debit. (*See 1 Peter 3:7*) God has given you your spouse on loan. He is waiting to see if they are returned better than He gave them to you or worse. What is God's ROI (return on investment) in our marriage?

The one who had received the five talents came up and
brought five more talents, saying, 'Master, you entrusted
five talents to me. See, I have gained five more talents.' His
master said to him, 'Well done, good and faithful slave. You
were faithful with a few things; I will put you in charge
of many things; enter into the joy of your master.'

MATTHEW 25:20-21

FAITH JOURNEY

Answering the Call Does Not Mean Easy Street

Being called by God does not guarantee things will be easy, but it will
be worth it. God will supply the strength and support necessary to
bring to fruit what He has planted in you and give you the resources
to accomplish what He is calling you to. Or said another way: As you
need it, the provision will be made available.

Mary, Jesus' mother, is the perfect example. "Greetings Favored One!
The Lord is with you!" (Luke 1:28) With this kind of annunciation
we could be tempted to believe that Mary was about to experience
nothing but favor and pleasantries for the rest of her life. What could
be a better mission than the mother of the Messiah? But scripture
records a few of Mary and Joseph's struggles, even while raising a
perfect son.

They were poor: The earliest evidence reflected a lack of earthly
means. Jesus was born in a stable and wrapped in cloth. Mary would
have known the time was close, so her preparation was to bring
the best option for the baby she could afford. On the eighth day,
Jesus was taken for circumcision according to the law. We are told
that they brought the required offering, two turtledoves, for the
purification rites. The ideal offering was a lamb, but if it couldn't

be afforded, the turtledoves were an acceptable substitute. (*See Leviticus 12:8.*) Joseph, as a carpenter, would not have been in the upper class of society.

Mary and Joseph worried about their son. Luke also records that even the perfect Son of Man caused His parents grief. After attending the Feast of the Passover in Jerusalem (they were devout Jews), Mary and Joseph left with the rest of their party, the caravan. But Jesus remained behind, spending three days (coincidence?) in the temple. (*See Luke 2:41-51*) When they finally realized Jesus had not joined the group, His parents went on a search for Him. They found Him learning and teaching in the temple. "Son, why have You treated us this way? Behold, your father and I have been anxiously looking for you!" (Luke 2:48b) Not even being in a synagogue is a good enough excuse to worry your parents.

If Mary was so favored and yet still had parenting heartaches raising a perfect Son, we must give ourselves and our children some grace. Our marriages, while divinely called, will still experience stress and difficulties. But the eternal impact is worth the effort.

"Therefore, the Lord Himself will give you a sign: Behold, the virgin will conceive and give birth to a son, and she will name Him 'Immanuel.'" (Isaiah 7:14)

The Best Reward for Our Time with God Is Time with God

PROSPERITY GOSPEL. THAT'S right, I went there. There is so much positioning on all sides of this doctrine — the belief emphasizes that Christians are ordained to be wealthy and healthy in this life and through eternity.

I know for a fact that God has great plans for me. (*See Jeremiah 29:11*) I know that I am the head and not the tail. (*See Deuteronomy 28:13*) But what is the prosperity that best brings the Kingdom of God here on earth?

God works all things for good for those who love him. (*See Romans 8:28*) But is there a way to live yielded to the Holy Spirit while keeping our minds on the things of heaven that bring about God's will in our lives and his purpose in our souls? Yes!

Paul is a great example of this. (Of course, Jesus is the perfect example.) Paul in his letters to the Philippians lays out a prosperity mindset that reflects the heart of Jesus. That is not to look at what is and isn't happening here on this earth, temporal treasures (*See Matthew 6:19*), but to look at what God's kingdom advancement might be in every situation. I mean, a good Father blesses His children, so my wants and needs here on earth are His pleasure to fulfill when they are a blessing for me. His ways are higher, so He knows the perfect resolution for my prayers—just as we imperfect parents can give our children what is good for them. We would not give our toddlers candy all day just because they demanded it. It would not be good parenting to do that. God is a perfect Father, and He answers my prayers perfectly.

If I am walking by the power of the Spirit, then what happens in the circumstances of my life is far less important than the eternal outcome that will be received. God will, for my benefit, withhold earthly treasures to steer me to greater riches. I cannot possibly know from my limited vantage point what the highest outcome is. I know in part. (1 Corinthians 13:12)

As I look to God as my heavenly Father, I need to posture my heart in thanksgiving and praise, because He is good. Because He always wants the very best for me, not just okay. If I truly yield to His authority, I am able to be content and even grateful no matter what the circumstance. (*See Philippians 4:12*) The mere process of attention toward asking of God and being in His presence is my reward. Receiving an audience with the King is the honor that elevates me, and I am rich having spent time in His courts.

When our focus becomes set on the things of this life, we miss the higher Kingdom good. Money is a tool; it is merely a training ground God can use to show me where my heart is and to teach me to be positioned toward heaven. Riches on earth are temporary and renewable, which makes them low-risk places to grow faith. Asking God only for earthly prosperity is very small thinking and does not reflect God's love for people. A marriage that values the things of the Kingdom of God will capture His heart.

But seek first His kingdom and His righteousness,
and all these things will be provided to you.

MATTHEW 6:33

Ingredients— Say You Are My Sister

Biblical Couple: Abram and Sarai

ABRAHAM IS CALLED the Father of Faith, but before he was elevated to that title he was known as Abram. This faith giant had to learn and grow his faith through trials and mistakes, just like we do. He and his wife, Sarah, even though they were a power couple, made more than their share of mistakes.

Twice as Abram and Sarai ventured to follow God's call, they encountered rulers that caused Abram to fear. "Tell them you are my sister." (Genesis 12:11-20 and Genesis 20) The Father of Faith sounds more like the Brother of Betrayal in these instances. The second time God had already given Abraham and Sarah their new identities and promised that they would have a child; it's hard to change our ways and live how God sees our character. Despite his fear and cowardice, God blesses Abraham through these trials. Each time he is given sheep and riches by the rulers he originally feared.

Abraham and Sarah divinely receive the promise of a son, but they are impatient in attempting to bring the promise to pass in their own strength. (Been there a time or two.) Sarah gives Abraham her maid, Hagar, to be the surrogate mother to the promised son. But God clearly spoke that the child would come through Sarah. Still, God brought His promise to pass and Sarai, now Sarah, is given a son in her old age. God is faithful even though we are not. We are not called when we are perfectly ready, but we are called when we are ready to be perfected.

FAITH JOURNEY

God Listens to Our Heart's Desires

Read Genesis 18:22-38

One of my favorite exchanges in the Bible is between Abraham and the angels who are about to destroy Sodom and Gomorrah. When Abraham learns what is about to happen, he fears for his nephew Lot. Abraham starts to bargain with the angels to spare Lot from destruction. The conversion starts with saving the city (if there are 50 righteous people, etc.), but Abraham realizes that the number is probably too high, so he auctions the angels down to five.

The next time you feel as if God has forgotten your request or that your plans are not important to God, just ask. Jesus taught us to ask so we could receive and seek so we can find. We need to in confidence ask and seek for the blessing and fullness God has for us. (*See Luke 11:13*)

ABRAHAM AND SARAH made many grave mistakes, but God blessed them despite their shortcomings. We need to continue to seek God's favor even though we are imperfect people. The enemy of our souls will attempt to keep us believing that we are not useful because of our past failures. That is simply not true.

Abraham and Sarah, looking at their human condition, could have started to believe that they were beyond the place where God could bring His promise through them. They were past their prime. God does not need our logic or even scientific evidence to bring His promises to pass. He calls us to participate in His great power made perfect in our inability to accomplish what only He can.

As Christians we must live in the richness of our salvation and forgiveness. When we sin or fall short, we need to repent and move on. Keeping a spirit of forgiveness in our marriages also enables us to stay healthy within our relationship. Knowing we are not perfect, and our spouse is not perfect, we should anticipate that mistakes and disappointments will happen — but we are learning and growing together.

In all of the instances we read of Abraham and Sarah, they remain committed to each other and the relationship. Their lack of good decision-making does not drive a wedge between them; they continue to walk out the promise one step at a time.

The Bible records the good and the bad of the people who make up its stories. God does not clean up or leave out the ugly truth. He uses their mistakes to teach us and showcase His great favor that He showed us in sending Jesus to die for our sins. We should use these examples to help us to avoid some of the pitfalls that they encountered without needing to make magnanimous mistakes like Abraham and Sarah did. We can learn from their shortcomings.

God's promises are sure; He will not leave them unanswered. We need to be patient with His timing and method for bringing them to pass. God is a good Father and wants good for His children and provides every means by which we can be successful in them. That's good parenting!

Living the Honeymoon Life

It needs to be differentiated here that we are not suggesting looking the other way or pretending that real issues will just go away. Mosaic Law gave allowance for divorce in cases where the covenant was broken by either party.

To those of you coming out of a marriage where you suffered from any of these conditions, our hearts break for you, and our prayer for your total restoration and healing is with you. Your marriage now does not reflect that past history or destine you in any way to be a statistic.

If your marriage shows any signs of needing mediation or professional help, it should be sought out. Your church may have resources. If that is too close for comfort, or one party is not engaged in that fellowship, there are plenty of commercial clinics where you can request counseling from someone of like faith.

Not long ago, Curtis and I had two blow-ups that caught us off-guard. We both were so shocked by how strong the emotions were that coincided with these moments that we decided to utilize the counseling service through his work. We were matched with a married Christian counselor. (We also believe your support person should have a successful relationship to be able to speak into your situation.) She offered us some great tools that we still utilize periodically to avoid major blow-ups. Some we have shared here.

We would further recommend that even if your marriage does not have deep wounds, you should still seek a couple more seasoned than you to mentor you. If you have a community that is supportive and worthy of emulation, you are very rich indeed!

Reflections for a Strong Marriage

"Look at the Mess We Started!"

Over a decade ago, my siblings and I threw our parents a surprise 50th anniversary party. My dad loved trains, so we took a little novelty three-hour train ride in Boone, Iowa. It included all three of us siblings, the six grandchildren, two sons-in-law, and my brother's pregnant girlfriend. The three of us decided we would pay for everything, which was a real stretch because my dad ALWAYS paid.

We purchased numerous tickets and had Mom and Dad board first to choose their spot. My older sister got on, then Curtis and I sat just in front of my parents. As the rest of the crew loudly entered the train, I sat facing my parents and thought, *Wow, I bet they are just overwhelmed that we pulled this off.* As our group finally finished boarding, my dad, with a twinkle in his eye, leaned over to my mom and said, "My God, look at the mess we started."

We have been quoting that line ever since. Anytime things get sideways in my family, I remind myself to have a little sense of humor about it. Taking too much credit or too much blame for the status of your children is just foolish. God, being the perfect Father, still had all of His children, except for Jesus, go astray. I wonder if God ever says to the Trinity, " My, 'Me,' look at the mess we started."

Waiting for God's Promise to Come to Pass

Perhaps like Curtis and me, you are still waiting for the fulfillment of a promise God has given you. As I mentioned, Curtis has a "Pray for Terri" alarm every day at 11:45 a.m. He utilizes that time to lift me up and sustain me in a list of items that are "Promises You (God) won't let Terri give up on." There are several that are related to our children and family, and some that are related to this next adventure, "Honeymoon Life," in which I am investing most of my efforts.

Having promises that are unfulfilled is not a lack of faith on your part or a lack of faithfulness on the Father's. These promises help us stay focused on God's purposes and His plans. Do not lose heart: If God has put something good in your heart, He will bring it to pass. The difficulty is trusting that we heard Him properly or that His timing is perfect. But let's take two examples from the Bible as a study in waiting on the Lord.

- Mary and Joseph took Jesus to be circumcised on the eighth day at the Temple in Jerusalem, to obey Jewish Law. For two individuals this routine occasion marked the fulfillment of a promise. They were looking for the promised Messiah to be revealed.

- Simeon: The Bible describes him as a "righteous and devout man, looking for the consolation of Israel; and the Holy Spirit was upon him." This man had been promised he would see the Messiah in the flesh before he died. Seeing Jesus, he blessed God for releasing him and gave a prophetic word to Mary and to "all those who were looking for the constellation of Israel." (Luke 2:25-27)

- Anna: She was eighty-four when she met Jesus. She had been widowed at a young age and had dedicated the rest of her life to temple service. She was a prophetess who "never left the temple, serving night and day with fasting and prayers." God rewarded her dedication by showing her the Messiah in the flesh. In her enthusiasm, she was sharing with everyone about him—"to all those who were looking for the redemption of Jerusalem." (Luke 2:36-38)

- Read the full account, Luke 2:21-38: Meeting the Savior of the World in the flesh was the highest reward these two dedicated souls lived for. We have a promise that Jesus is coming back to take us home. We must live our lives looking for the second coming of our Savior.

What's in a Name—Terri Means "Harvester"

WHILE GROWING UP, I did not like my name. I had asked my parents at one point how they came up with it. The response was: "It was a character on a soap opera." I pressed, "Was she a good character? Someone you liked?" "Not really," my mom replied. So much for answers.

I always felt like my name, and perhaps my person, was just not that big of a deal. I kind of had a sadness in my spirit about it. Fast-forward to Maui, around 2009. I was dancing with the Hula Ministry and our *kumu* (teacher) gave us a homework assignment. Share the meaning of your name. (These ladies were dedicated students of the Word!)

Great, I thought, *this will be a moment of sharing my childhood pain.* I researched to the best of my ability at that time and found what I had found before; derived from Theresa. At our next gathering, others began sharing the lovely meanings of their names. Hawaiian names are long and rich and have deep meaning. The spellings can be complicated and difficult to pronounce, but I have not met many locals on the Islands who did not know why they received their name. It is a big part of the culture. I was getting a little nervous thinking about how I would admit that my name really had no meaning, no significance. But before I could take my turn, my *kumu* spoke up and said, "This is kind of strange, but I have a word for Terri. Your name means harvester! I looked it up and it does!"

Tears began to roll down my cheeks. I felt a welling up inside me that I cannot describe. Suddenly my personality and abilities made sense to me. The character traits I was not appreciating about myself gave new purpose to who I was as a child of God. Even the fact that I am an avid gardener. I was significant. My parents may not have known why, but they had obediently listened to the Holy Spirit, and I was given a beautiful name that is precious to me today. God gave me decades to ponder the meaning and purpose behind my name. I was ready to live disheartened and give in to the lie that I was nothing special and that my own parents had not put thought into naming me. But the reality that my Heavenly Father had placed great significance on me and put all of the talents into me that He would require of me still makes me tear up.

Men, This Relates to You: Say My Name

Men don't tend to get emotional about their names. However, all of our brains react positively when we hear others speak our name. Studies prove that we are hardwired to feel comfort and joy when we hear our own name.[10] If you don't know so already, your value as an individual is worth dying for to Jesus. We must embrace that even the hairs on our head, though that number may be in decline, are counted by our heavenly Father. (*See Matthew 10:30*)

Ladies, if you are not already doing so, try a slow, soft whisper in his ear, calling him by name. You may be surprised how much of a deposit into his love tank this can be.

It's Biblical

In the Bible, especially the Old Testament, the naming of a child was culturally very important. Many times, the Bible records that angels directly deliver the name a child is to receive before they are born. When Naomi lost her husband and her sons, she changed her own name to Mara, meaning bitter. (*See Ruth 1:20*) In Revelation we are told that God records the names of His children, you and me, in the Lamb's Book of Life. (*See Revelation 20:15*) If you are struggling to embrace how precious you are, and how much your Heavenly Father has poured out to spend eternity with you, just remember your name is written down—like a family photo album for our Heavenly Father to relish. So, God Himself is saying our names. Jesus will come back to all who put our faith in Him and call us by name.

Living the Honeymoon Life

We have shared in this book that as our children grew up, there were seasons of difficulty. We happily share that today we are united in love once again. Working on this book has helped reveal how much healthier our relationships are. We spent several days testing the recipes contained in this book. Phoebe, "Max," and Alex made several batches of the no-bake cookies, which meant there was a lot of sampling that needed done. They came up with a product idea in the process.

Victoria made two batches of schnitzel, one of pork and then a few days later, chicken. The recipe is laborious, and she spent hours in the kitchen. She only requested assistance on the cleanup and occasional watching of a pan as she took a needed momentary break. She also made her famous red cabbage to complement the dish.

I made my deviled eggs, which were consumed within a matter of an hour.

Curtis was resident food taster and cleanup crew, as was one of our grandsons.

Of course, we all gathered at the table each time a dish was completed. I am happy to report that I have been officially dethroned when it comes to many family recipes, but I gladly pass on the baton! That is truly living the Honeymoon Life, when your children and their children take part in the responsibility and execution of a family goal, like writing this book. God is good all the time, and all the time God is good!

Family Recipes

IN A LARGE family like the one Curtis grew up in, getting your favorite meal was on special occasions only. He requested pork chops for his birthday meal, plain fried pork chops with applesauce on the side. For dessert, it was pound or lemon cake. A few years ago, our second daughter, who is our resident chef, made his childhood favorites for his birthday. He was so blessed by her gesture. For just a moment, he did not miss his mom as much.

Pork Chops with Pineapple   Bonnie Krupp

Bread pork chops and fry until golden brown Place in baking pan On each chop place a ring of pineapple and pour pineapple juice over,
Bake ¾ to 1 hour.
When ready to serve, place a cherry in center of pineapple

Glazed Pork Roast

Place pork roast fat side down in shallow pan Roast at 350°, 45 to 50 minutes per lb.

Apricot Glaze

½ cup apricot preserves
2 tsp. dry mustard.
2 tsp. lemon juice

Combine preserve, mustard and juice. Mix thoroughly. During last 20 or 30 minutes of roasting pork, spread glaze over roast. Return to oven, finish roasting.

Schnitzel Recipe by Victoria

Schnitzel Recipe by Victoria

4 pounds of chicken or pork	Water or milk to mix w/eggs
½ Tablespoon garlic powder	2 cups flour
1 Tablespoon salt	½ Tablespoon onion powder
3 cups panko	½ Tablespoon pepper
4 eggs	1 teaspoon paprika
High-temp oil	

1. Trim excess fat if needed. Depending on your meat and how it was cut when you bought it, you'll cut the chicken or pork into about 1-inch-thick pieces. Then, using the smooth side of a mallet, beat your protein into 1/4-inch-thick pieces. (I place the piece between two sheets of plastic wrap to cut down on the mess.) Try to keep the pieces even, so the cooking process is also easier.

2. Once you have your meat prepared, season your flour and panko with the seasonings listed to your preferred taste. (I season by feeling and personal preference.) You should see some color change and be able to smell the seasonings in the plate or dish big enough to hold the whole flat piece of pork or chicken.

3. Crack and beat the eggs in a separate dish. (Add a little milk or water to your eggs if you prefer.)

4. Then, in an assembly line fashion, bread the protein in flour, then egg, and then panko, and set to the side. Continue the process until all of your meat is properly breaded.

5. In a deep pan, add in your choice of oil, enough for the schnitzel to swim in it, and bring up to temp. To check if your oil is hot enough without a thermometer, take a little pinch of the flour or panko and put it in the oil. If it bubbles immediately, your oil is ready. (Note that during the cooking process, oil temperature will lower and rise in accordance with the stage of cooking. Adjust heat as necessary to avoid oil "smoking" or cooling too much.)

6. Add in your meat, making sure not to crowd the pan, and fry until golden brown, about 2-3 minutes on each side. Set cooked pieces on either a slotted tray or a plate with a paper towel to soak up excess oil. Then you're done.

7. Our family likes to serve with brown mushroom gravy and spaetzle for Jaeger Schnitzel.

The making of our Jaeger Family Schnitzel Recipe

Beating the Odds

If you are reading this, chances are you are still married and working to improve it. The highest population for divorce in our country right now is people over 50 who have been in relationships for 20 years or more—the epidemic of Gray Divorce I mentioned earlier.

Let's go back. Christian married couples, the standard for our union is the original design of marriage in the Garden of Eden in communion with God. We are here on this earth to learn to look like Jesus and His Bride, the Church. What if instituting a few habits that are inexpensive and do not require a lot of time could save you decades of investment in your marriage? Many we are sharing with you in this book.

Curtis and I have known more than our share of stress in our marriage. From the very beginning when we were stationed in Europe far away from families, we realized that to survive as a couple we were going to need to rely on each other. We decided to get out of the Air Force to give our marriage top priority. (Hats off to all of you who made marriage work and stayed on active duty. Ladies and gentlemen, that is not an easy task!)

We got married and had four children. Learning to navigate marriage, parenting, careers, layoffs, moving several times, mortgages, and extended family has proven to be a tightrope walk. But it is also what makes up our story as a couple. These challenges and trials not only forced us to work as a team but also taught us to rely more deeply on God.

As Christians, we should not fall prey to the lie that "the grass is greener on the other side," that we might be better off as a single person, or with a younger/different spouse. God brought you and your spouse together as an opportunity for you to bring out the best in each other. To return them better than you received them. If you plant daily into your marriage, you will reap a harvest that yields bountiful fruit. Your marriage must be a testimony to the mystery of God's great love for people. It proves that He desires to have relationships with us.

FUN & GAMES

Teaching an Old Dog New Tricks

Staying interested in each other is not that difficult. Curtis and I keep learning about each other and new things all the time. With the advent of YouTube, the possibilities are endless, and accessibility is free. You can find just about anything you are interested in. Each of you should list possible activities you have wanted to try. Where these lists overlap, you have your first venture. If none of them match, take a look at the activities you have come up with, taking into account both your physical condition and energy levels.

Perhaps there is a family reunion in the mountains; perhaps you could look up some fly-fishing tips or learn to tie flies. Or make a schedule to get into hiking shape, starting small and working up to your target hike. Of course, a hike up a mountain is more strenuous than sea level, so give yourselves some leeway in the planning.

Maybe you have a mission trip to Mexico. Learning Spanish online or a phone app could help bridge some awkward moments and possibly keep you out of trouble. Honestly and thankfully, Curtis learned enough Italian and knew enough German to get us out of some scrapes.

Is there a wedding on the calendar? If you are one of those couples who sit at the table while your friends are out on the dance floor, start with dance lessons. You can find all activity levels and styles online. Start small and master two or three moves; consistently practicing those can give you confidence and class on the dance floor. Note here, ladies: If you have not partner-danced before, the gentleman leads. Once you resign to it, you are going to love how he shows up for you.

Make it relevant and start small. We committed to practicing 15 minutes per day five days per week while we took dance lessons. The opportunity to find a new hobby to do together is worth every effort, and you will reap lifetime rewards for your effort.

Living the Honeymoon Life

In order to reap, we must sow. One of our go-to habits is texting each other throughout the day. We use it as an opportunity to flirt and keep the time apart interesting. This quick and free effort yields excitement and anticipation for the end of the day when we are back together. Think of it as a little mood-setter, a little foreplay. Even if it does not always end in intimacy, when you do get around to having it, I guarantee that you will be in the mood for it.

"Waste Not, Want Not"

That old adage is so relevant to life. We invest our adult lives into working, raising a family, our marriage, and hopefully habits that keep us healthy. When we get to the Autumn season of our lives and marriages, we should continue to pour the same amount of energy into it. It would be a shame if we didn't harvest all the good things we have worked for.

The concept of "dying on the vine" states that fruit that is not utilized is useless. If for instance you work hard at a job your entire life but find that when the time comes to step back from the daily grind you are unhappy and feel as if you are no longer needed, that is a lie. You have a lot to offer the future, and if you are still passionate about your career field there are plenty of opportunities to mentor the next generation. You can do it formally or informally.

In your marriage, you navigated all that life threw at you together, then when it comes time for you to enjoy some time together, but you can't find things you enjoy together, that is a waste. Extra time easily goes to grandkids and more serving in the church but set aside time for just the two of you and enjoy all that you have stored up.

Perhaps time and money are no longer a valid excuse *not* to do something. Take one of your bucket list trips or purchase that classic car you both have always wanted. These can be great ministry opportunities as well. For example, at our planned car shows, I intend to advertise free prayer.

Autumn should be a time for harvesting and sharing what we find in abundance. I mentioned earlier that while growing up in Iowa, the final harvest meant time canning and freezing for the winter. We also spent time baking squash into breads and cookies and "putting up" root vegetables for storage. The items that we had in too much abundance went to neighbors. Our marriage activities during Autumn can be this kind of blessing.

CURTIS' INPUT

Yes, Ma'am

When we lived in Sigourney, Iowa, from 1995 to 2003, it was like Mayberry to me. The population was 2,200 and stable. It was a typical midwestern small town. The only time we locked our doors was at night. Neighbors were friendly, and everyone knew your business. At first, it was a bit weird coming from metropolitan areas in California and Colorado. I soon got used to it and then embraced it. We lived in an old Victorian home on a little less than half-acre. We had plum, cherry, apple, and pear trees. Terri had a "little" garden out back. There were neighborhood kids every which way. An eighty-year-old lady, Lydia, lived behind us in a Victorian house on several acres. She was like a grandma to us and was unafraid to help us or ask for help. It was what being neighbors was about! Life was really idyllic.

Well, Lydia had an overbearing seventy-year-old cousin, Colleen, who enjoyed explaining to me the ins and outs of trees, other plants, vehicles, responsibility, and anything else she could think of. Mind you, I wasn't annoyed; it was just odd that this person I had no real connection with had decided to impart her wisdom on me. Terri would always chuckle when I would walk in from a one-sided discussion with Colleen.

One Indian Summer, I heard a knock on the back door. Lo and behold, it was Colleen. I opened the door and said, "Come on in! Good to. . ."

"I ain't coming in—you need to come outside," Colleen stated emphatically.

"I guess we are going outside," I said. My snarkiness didn't bother her.

"Come here," she said, a bit perturbed. "Are you going to let those pears rot on the tree? That would be a waste. There isn't a pear tree in town that has that much fruit! It would be a shame to let it all go to waste!" Not much of that fruit ever went to waste. True, it was the most bountiful pear tree in town, but what we didn't use, we either stored or gave away.

"Yeah, I was going to. . ." I tried telling her that I had already planned on picking the pears in a day or two. But she was on a mission.

"Now go get a ladder. I will back up my truck, and we will get all the fruit down today."

For the next hour or so, Colleen directed me on pear picking. "We" picked every piece of fruit off that overly full pear tree. Bags and bags of some of the best pears I have ever had. After I put the ladder away, Colleen and I looked at the multitude of bags of pears in the back of her truck. She didn't act impressed, but I sure was. This was great!

Then she asked," So, are you guys going to eat any of these, or should I just take them all?"

She was stepping on toes now. I wasn't sure if she thought that she was doing me a favor by taking the pears or if she was just being, well, herself. But she did seem a bit surprised by my answer.

"Colleen, I have a growing family, as you know. We pick these pears from August until November. Terri likes them better in August; I prefer the November version. But we won't let any of these go to waste. Why don't you take whatever you are going to eat, and a bag or two for Lydia. We will make good use of the rest. Terri makes a great pear chutney, some get stored in the cellar, and the kids love them as well."

She was a bit speechless—for a brief moment. "Well, that sounds like a good plan! Do you need help bringing them into the house?"

"No, but thank you, Colleen. I will get Terri and the kids to help me. Thanks for helping me get all those pears picked!"

Autumn brings back wonderful memories.

Fresh Starts and Do-Overs

Created in His Image—To Love as He Loves

HAVE YOU EVER heard someone say they are trying to find the meaning of life? "Why am I here?" These questions can become a pursuit of self-fulfillment and enlightenment: Could life be more purposeful and impactful than just the discovery of why we exist?

Jesus gives insight into God's value system for what we invest our time and resources into. His disciples asked Him about the timing of the return of His kingdom and His ascent to power. They were looking for the fulfillment of His earthly reign and the return of Israel to glory. In response, Jesus gives His disciples several parables to help them understand that the focus of our lives here on earth is to be preparing for eternity. (For further understanding, *see Matthew 24-25*)

Making eternal investments should be a priority in every Christian's life. Jesus describes final judgment as us standing before a King on His throne. He will consider our actions, the things we have done to our fellowman, as proof of our faith. We are saved by grace, and no work we do can add to the value of that; we are obligated to pursue the Father's heart while here on earth. "But are you willing to acknowledge, you foolish person, that faith without works is useless?" (James 2:20)

So how do we meet the burden of a world that has such great needs? Where we can. It's that simple. Let us stop using the excuse that there is just too much to be done and start doing it. Jesus identified six demographics where we are expected to meet needs. In the parable, both the saints and the sinners exclaim "when did we see you. . ." God puts those in your path He expects you to exercise mercy on.

- **Hungry:** Perhaps there is an elderly neighbor or a single mother in your sphere of influence. If not, food banks are in desperate need of donations. Additionally, there is always the option to volunteer at a soup kitchen. Most school districts now allow a student's school lunch debt to be paid off by others. So, if you don't personally know someone in need you can still feed others.

- **Thirsty:** You can carry water bottles in your car to pass out to those you see begging or to anyone who might benefit from clean, fresh water. Also, there are organizations that bring fresh water to those around the world who do not otherwise have access. Our favorite: The Bucket Ministry (https://thebucketministry.org/). For a mere $50 you can ensure a family has access to clean water for life, plus necessary medications to clear up the issues that came from drinking the tainted water. They also receive the Gospel in a close and personal way.

- **Naked:** Donate the clothes you don't wear. Many school districts and churches now have specific items they ask for to help with prom, going back to work, or other life event needs. You could always organize a clothes swap within your friends' group; everyone gets a new look without spending a penny. (How about an ugly Christmas sweater exchange?!)

- **Stranger:** Sit next to the new person in church or in the Break Room who is sitting alone. Attempt to start a conversation.

- **Sick:** Take meals to the family, send cards of encouragement, or visit if it is an option. (When my friend, who lived 35 minutes away without traffic was dying of cancer, I would send DoorDash funds to them. Easy for me and they could be used as the need arose, getting just what they wanted, no fridge space needed.)

- **In Prison:** There is a great organization called Prison Fellowship Angel Tree that supports the children of inmates and gives that parent credit and an opportunity to interact in the gift exchange. Your church may participate, if not find them online. (https://www.prisonfellowship.org/about/angel-tree/)

"When the Son of Man comes in His glory, and all the angels with Him, then He will sit on His glorious throne" (Matthew 25:31). He will separate us as sheep and goats according to our deeds. The quality that will prove us to be true followers of Christ is how we took care of the people God put in our path—our generosity and compassion to our fellow traveler. God will weigh what we did with our time and energy and resources that benefited others, especially those who were not able to provide for themselves.

The "least of these" are the people in our lives who have a need, who are lost and need direction. When we meet a brother or sister in a difficult situation it is our opportunity to give them the water that they are thirsty for. If you haven't identified anyone to help, just pray that God will reveal them to you. One of the most satisfying activities you can do with your spouse is serving people who cannot possibly repay you.

> And the King will answer and say to them, "Truly I say to you, to the extent you did it to one of these brothers or sisters of Mine, you did it to me.
>
> **MATTHEW 25:40**

WORK IT OUT TOGETHER

Finding Balance in Each Stage of Life—Reinforce Memory Verse

Therefore, we do not lose heart, but though our outer person is decaying, yet our inner *person* is being renewed day by day.

2 CORINTHIANS 4:16 Having a plan set in stone with little deviation is great on paper (or well, in stone), but the reality is that there is not one perfect schedule that will accommodate every stage of life. Our physical abilities and energy changes. Our financial margin changes. Our interests also grow and die. Respecting this stage as new territory instead of continuing down the same old rutted path is God honoring. That is why check-ins are crucial to keep the marriage heading toward God's ultimate plan. Like financial budget meetings, course corrections, as we studied in spring, are necessary to ensure that time, money, and energy are allocated properly to maximize the return on investment.

Empty nesting can also be called a second shot at "just the two of us." DATING! Make your schedules and budget fit where you are today. Remove any activities that are left just because "we have always done it that way." If they are no longer serving their purpose, they need to go. Add activities and commitment that remind you how blessed you are and reward you for "time served" in your life sentence of marriage.

This stage of life will still have its demands and issues, so continuing your habits of check-ins is necessary. If there are still touchy subjects or pet peeves between spouses, these meetings can serve as great resolution moments. For example, being prompt to appointments and commitments: Is he a "15 minutes early is on time" guy, while she is a "fashionably late is in fashion" gal? These differing points of view can be stumbling blocks that impede our ability to fight harmoniously side by side; they need to be worked out. Our check-ins can serve as healing moments and add understanding.

Curtis and I like to use drive time during a day trip or commitments as preliminary meetings. I take notes on my phone of our conversations. I sometimes email those notes to us so we can review separately, make adjustments by email correspondence, then get together for a follow-up meeting. Sometimes, that calls for another road trip; just saying!

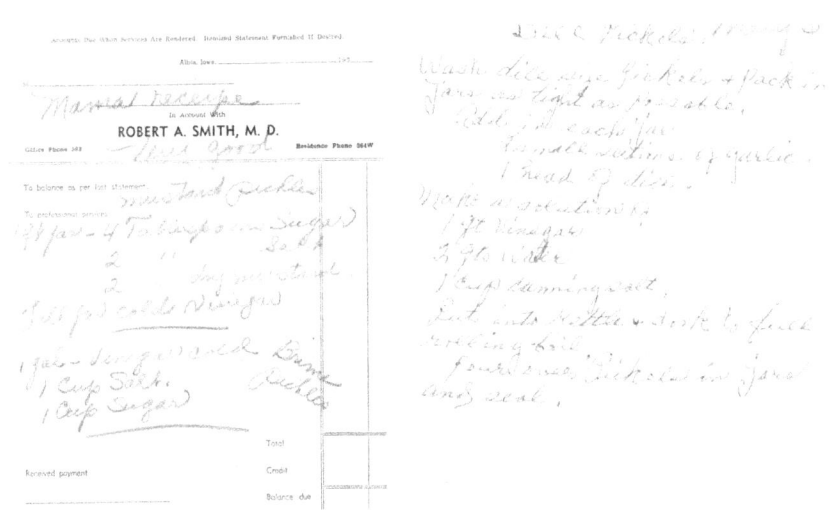

Dueling recipes from Grandma Isabell and Great Aunt Mary

MY GREAT AUNT Mary and my Grandmother Isabell were always competing. When they played music together, it was more like dueling pianos than a harmonious duet. When it came to the kitchen, the rivalry really heated up (pun intended).

I found this example in one of my Grandmother Isabell's canning cookbooks. The front of the recipe in Mary's handwriting was a truncated recipe for their mother's mustard pickles. It must have been Mary's way to "give but not give" her baby sister the recipe of pickles that their mother had handed down.

I can picture Grandma pestering Mary about the details and the process to make these memorable delicacies. Then alas, in my Grandma Johnson's handwriting, the back side of the recipe shows the details that Isabell eventually got from Mary, for Mary's Dill Pickles. I wonder if Grandma ever got the Mustard Pickle details? I don't recall her ever making them. I am so grateful she got this recipe; we have since made these pickles for many years from the abundance of harvest in our gardens. These ladies were salty in many ways!

"You are the salt of the earth; but if the salt has become tasteless, how can it be made salty again? It is no longer good for anything, except to be thrown out and trampled underfoot by people."

MATTHEW 5:13

Krupp Marriage Experience

An Autumn in Our Marriage Is Just Beginning

AT THE TIME of this writing, Curtis is still working full-time. I am dedicating the majority of my energy to prayer and study and delivering the message of the Honeymoon Life to those who God intends to receive it. Our children are adults, and we find ourselves with the opportunity to do things as we desire.

We have planned and mapped out what we assumed we wanted this time of our lives to look like, but we still find that some of our expectations and assumptions need fine-tuning. We happily work to get the most out of the time we find ourselves in, but we refuse to allow it to be a time of sitting on our laurels. We intend to squeeze every bit of life out of the time we have left. Like many people, we have a bucket list that we hope to accomplish and experience. For us, it continues to grow. God has not called us out to pasture; He's called us up to the next level.

Autumn for us is shaping up into a time of reflection, harvesting, and sharing of our bounty. It is such a blessing to wake up every day and see my best friend right there beside me. It is such a great comfort to know that we are more committed and dedicated to our wedding vows than the day we made them.

Autumns can come throughout your marriage. The moments between the ending of one season and the beginning of another often offer a small chance to breathe and embrace all that you have accomplished in the past, while looking forward to what the future brings.

SALT AND LIGHT

DON'T Give Up

When it comes to making things last, salt is the world's oldest and most frequently used element, especially in preserving food. God wants to use your marriage to preserve His plans here on earth. Don't withhold any of the recipe that will make it easy for others to see your love and know that it is Christ in you giving you strength. Risk: Put it all out there! Live up to your Priscilla and Aquila potential!

Living out your marriage daily as an act of worship and love for your creator and savior shines bright in this world of apathy. Finding the romance in God's calling and your marriage mission affects everyone around you. You are the Salt of the Earth and a Light to the World.

It may be tempting to sit back and relax from all the work you have put in when you feel Autumn in the air. The temptation to retire and slow down is strong as our bodies and relationships feel the effects of time and season as they pass. But God is not done with your marriage yet. He is giving us this time to refuel but keep the momentum going.

"Do nothing from selfishness or empty conceit, but with humility consider one another as more important than yourselves; do not *merely* look out for your own personal *interests*, but also for the *interests* of others."

PHILIPPIANS 2:3-4

When It Comes to Winter, Everyone Should Be a Boy Scout

Times of ease, like Autumn, can give us a false sense of security. If we begin to believe we will continue to float through peaceful seasons, we may under-appreciate that Winter, bitter trials of life, can be waiting just around the corner. Like getting ready for a day in the snow, hats, mittens, coats, and boots must be acquired. Enduring Winter difficulties should be met by donning the spiritual armor of God.

Living the Honeymoon Life

Attributes of love, as detailed in I Corinthians 13, may seem like no-brainers in marriage. But applying these virtues proves to be a challenge, and I have glaring weaknesses. One of my shortcomings is "Love is not self-seeking."

At first glance within a marriage, it would be easy to dismiss this characteristic of love. I mean, we live together and have a joint checking account. We sit on the couch and watch Netflix. How could I be self-seeking in my marriage?

I have discovered that self-seeking rears its ugly head in so many ways. One way I have been self-seeking is that I tend to plan something for every minute of Curtis' waking hours. I have agreed to outings before consulting with him, and I have signed up for classes and seminars for us that he doesn't truly get the chance to say no to because he has always been such a good sport. I am self-seeking.

My thoughts, plans, and ideas took precedence, and I rarely considered the ramifications on Curtis. He finally spoke up not long ago and admitted, "I'm tired. We are constantly doing something." I heard him and I listened. I immediately canceled a few non-critical commitments. I rearranged some appointments to leave breathing room in our schedule. I stepped back and looked at how I had been strong-arming our calendar, and I repented to him in sincere apology. It has breathed life into our relationship and has been a very welcomed change.

The takeaway for me: Before I consider anything that would require Curtis' time and energy or take me away from our time, I must base my decision on my love for my spouse. It has been a pivotal moment in our relationship, giving romance and tenderness the time it deserves.

WINTER

PENGUINS

While not all penguin species live in Antarctica, the majority of them do. The lack of land predators in extreme conditions makes a flightless bird less at risk. They are perfectly suited (pardon the pun) for these extreme conditions: Their bodies are covered in oil-sealed, overlapping feathers that cause internal heat to be maintained even amid the harshest cold temperatures. These creatures will huddle close together to guard against cold and wind. Many species of penguins are known to mate for life, and even "mourn" the loss of a mate.

THOUGH IT OFTEN brings severe weather, the benefit of winter to the earth is a relief and rest from expending energy during the growing season. Winter is a time for the earth to renew the much-needed nutrients in the soil, usually through tumultuous events like plants dying, leaves falling, and other decay.

It may be that you reached for this book when you were looking for hope and encouragement. Perhaps you have recently experienced some bad news, loss, or great pain in your family, and you are finding it very difficult to make the adjustments to remain in unison with your spouse. In this book, I have called this season of bitterness Winter. This season of extreme conditions can cause us to grow cold toward each other.

When we face these harsh conditions in our lives and marriages, how will we respond? Will we allow the bitterness of the season to sink deep into our hearts and turn us away from each other? Or can we insulate ourselves by putting on our Spiritual Armor to guard our hearts and minds, no matter what is happening around us?

WINTER

The Season

A Winter Challenge in My Parents' Marriage

MY DAD WAS a chain smoker in my young life until I was about eight. He smoked in the car, in his office (which was in our home at the time)—just about anywhere he was, except church and his mom's house. Then he developed a bad cough, so he visited the doctor. The doctor gave him an ultimatum: "Stop smoking or die." That was all it took. My dad, per my mom's account, walked out of the doctor's office, dropping his last pack of cigarettes in the trash, and never smoked again. The withdrawal must have been awful, but because of his commitment to his family, he knew that he really had no other choice. With our mother's support, he stayed smoke-free the rest of his life.

It is not easy to maintain our peace in the face of adversity, but we are made to do hard things. Let's not give up when the challenge of Winter is upon us. The key is to face these storms and seasons in unity and agreement with our spouse. We can allow it to be a catalyst for joining us in holy oneness with our spouse, cleaving us together as God ordained in the Garden of Eden. If we are asking God for His help together in our oneness and united in Him, that is His will for us. Our memory verse gives us confidence in asking in agreement with our spouse, and for the glory of God will not go unheard.

Scripture to Memorize Together

This is the confidence which we have before Him, that, if
we ask anything according to His will, He hears us.

1 JOHN 5:14

 **FAITH JOURNEY**

You are Leading a Tiny Congregation in Your Home—Your Family

"Again, truly I tell you, that if two of you on earth
agree about anything they ask, it will be done by
my Father in heaven. For where two or three are
gathered in my name, there I am in their midst"

MATTHEW 18:19-20

Initially, I wanted to utilize this verse as the memory verse. But I sought wisdom and asked for feedback on use of scripture. This verse is considered misused in the context of every gathering of Christians.

This promise was given to the disciples in regard to church discipline. While most of us have quoted this verse for use with any gathering of believers, it seems to be directed toward official transactions within the body. However, you and your spouse are managing a small congregation, your family, even if it just you and your spouse. Coming together in boldness of grace because Jesus made a way for our salvation, and in unity of agreement, God honors your prayers.

Prayerfully consider your spouse and yourself as leaders of the calling God has placed on your marriage.

WINTER SEASONS, LIKE my childhood winters growing up in Iowa, can seem to take forever to end. While the initial snowfall can be beautiful to behold, the ensuing dirty slush makes the roadways and sidewalks ugly and causes cars to become packed with dingy ice. The danger of slipping on "black ice" (hidden patches of ice that closely resemble the surrounding medium) is highest during the coldest hours. You cannot fight the cold alone, unprotected, and survive.

A marriage going through a harsh season—let's say with rebellious teenagers—can be at risk of being pulled down into strife. To make it through these hard times, we must first practice unity before we are fit to fight the good fight, side by side. That way, instead of sinking into the mire with them, you are strongly unified as a couple, and you are able to raise them up to a solid footing with you.

Paul teaches on harmony and unity, children obeying parents, and fathers treating their children with respect. Later, we see him write on the hierarchy of husbands and wives. The order of leadership and respect makes and breaks a family, or any organization.

"Children, obey your parents in the Lord, for this is right. Honor your father and mother (which is the first commandment with a promise), so that it may be well with you, and that you may live long on the earth. Fathers do not provoke your children to anger but bring them up in the discipline and instruction of the Lord. Slaves, be obedient to those who are your masters according to the flesh, with fear and trembling, in the sincerity of your heart, as to Christ; not by way of eye service, as men-pleasers, but as slaves of Christ, doing the will of God from the heart. With goodwill render service, as to the Lord, and not to men, knowing that whatever good thing each one does, this he will receive back from the Lord, whether slave or free. And masters, do the same things to them, and give up threatening, knowing that both their Master and yours is in heaven, and there is no partiality with Him." (Ephesians 6:1-9)

The order is for subordinates to honor those in charge, and for leaders to remember they are both under God's orderly command equally. It is noteworthy that the subordinate children and servants are instructed first. The positions of parents and leaders are, by design, due respect. Then he addresses the authority, saying that these positions of power are not to be of abuse, but of loving guidance. Harmony and unity within the unit must first be established; then, the training for battle can begin. This Godly alignment of authority in the home and in fair marketplace treatment is crucial to being able to fight the true battle. This is true in our marriage as well. We must be ordered in a Godly fashion as well to ensure we have protection during the battle.

CURTIS' INPUT

"Be Prepared" Is Not Just for Boy Scouts

People who could quote scripture always amazed me. I couldn't understand how they could remember all those verses. Well, we were living in Oahu and fellowshipping at New Hope in Honolulu. The pastor, Wayne Cordero, had a way of reaching people through an easygoing vibe and stories of growing up as a Portuguese kid in Hawaii.

During one service he rattled off like ten verses to answer questions a non-believer might ask. Not only was it an impressive display, it moved me to start memorizing verses that not only spoke to me but could help Christians and non-Christians alike.

I started memorizing scripture around 2006-07. It started with some simple, easy-to-memorize verses. Over the years I have memorized twenty-five to thirty that I recite on my daily morning walk. Some days they really speak to me. They lift my spirit, and they convict me. Mainly, I just want to be prepared for that person whom God sends my way who needs to hear His Word.

Basic Training—Taking the "I" Out of Team

AS AN EIGHTEEN-YEAR-OLD in the Air Force, I completed basic training. It was our "boot camp." This intense orientation is the foundation for making a "combat-ready" flight. At its core, it is designed to allow a unit of mixed backgrounds and skillsets to work in unison. Separated by gender, we learned Air Force history and trained in military life, physical fitness, basic war skills, and chemical, biological, radiological, and nuclear warfare. This stage of training prepares the airmen to act and work uniformly, from the cadence of the march in formation to setting aside personal comfort and making decisions based on what's best for the mission overall. For example, if one airman from the flight commits a serious-enough offense, the entire flight loses liberties.

One of the common tests of preparedness was door guard duty. In this exercise, the order is given to the door guard that no unauthorized personnel, even training instructors (TIs), are allowed into the dorm, and even then, only with them producing proper identification. This scenario was tested on many nights throughout the course. The scene goes like this: Late at night, a scared, little no-rank airman is on post at the door of the dormitory where all their fellow flight members are sleeping. An unauthorized TI shows up, pounding on the locked door, screaming, insisting on being let in, refusing to show the proper identification. They lie, threaten, and posture to make this poor airman almost wet themselves, but the point of the drill is clear: "No unauthorized personnel, no matter their rank, is let in."

The door and the under-ranking individual guarding it have dominion over the higher-ranking intruder. It is all a game, of course, but when you are barely eighteen and facing down this very scary superior, screaming at the top of their lungs and threatening you, there is a temptation to question your original orders. I am happy to report that I stood firm the night this happened on my watch. In this case, we were rewarded when the airman stood her ground and followed orders properly.

CURTIS' INPUT

Air Force Training, Sir!

I also remember door guard duty, and my experience didn't occur or end without drama. When I was assigned to watch another flight's entry door, I was framed. I had the door open to allow the airmen to enter as they walked up the stairs. As the forty or so airmen entered the room, I was eyeing the stairs to avoid being tricked. One airman said that there were about ten guys left, and they started to trickle in kind of sporadically. He said the TI was behind them. At least that is what I thought he said. Well, after about seven or eight entered, the TI jumped from behind the door and stuck his foot in the door as I was slamming it.

He was undaunted. I was daunted. I wouldn't let him in no matter what he said, and he wouldn't move his foot no matter what I said. He won. I had to be retrained. He never explained what I was supposed to do. My own TI never told me what I was supposed to do. And at the training, I posed the question to them, and they didn't give me an answer. I just messed up, and that is all I needed to know.

THE DEVIL, THE enemy of your eternal soul, is a master at playing these mind games. He can take your best and most intimate protection layer between you and your spouse and make it appear that you are opponents. Yet, like training to become one military unit, spouses in a marriage must work to be solidified under truth and protection of God's armor. Unification is the strong foundation in teamwork necessary to ensure you can face battles together.

A marriage must work as a complement of forces, especially during difficult or bitter moments. This can be done by establishing a unified purpose: We are the Air Force of God. To accomplish the mission's purpose, Paul turns his attention to the reality of the fight: spiritual warfare.

> Finally, be strong in the Lord and in the strength of His might. Put on the full armor of God, so that you will be able to stand firm against the schemes of the devil. For our struggle is not against flesh and blood, but against the rulers, against the powers, against the world forces of this darkness, against the spiritual forces of wickedness in the heavenly places.

EPHESIANS 6:10-12

Don't miss what Paul is doing here: It may be difficult to focus when you are in a cold and bitter season, but know that your true enemy is the devil, not each other. The war is not between you and your spouse. The struggle is not between you and your children. The tension is not because of your boss, in-laws, or even the disease you are fighting. It is the devil. Once you are focused on being readied in God's basic training, your enemy will become clear and you can focus all of your efforts on fighting the battle, side by side, in harmony with your closest ally, your spouse!

Christian marriages hold a powerful opportunity to take back our families, neighborhoods, churches, and towns to the glory of God. But we must be in agreement to accomplish anything. Often, we are busy focusing on our spouse's shortcomings or past hurts, so the potential to be unified gets moved out of the focal point. God is calling your marriage to rise up! If you are reading this, God is on the move in your marriage. He is calling your marriage to represent him and take back the power that seems to be taken from you but is truly endowed within you. Remember, two or more—you and your spouse in agreement—moves the heavens!

I am not afraid of an army of lions led by a sheep; I am afraid of an army of sheep led by a lion.

ALEXANDER THE GREAT

The Struggle Is Real

Conversely, the devil hates you and will work hard to ensure you never meet your full potential as individuals and certainly not as a couple. The very first marriage in the Garden of Eden started a war between humans and the devil. The deceiver will work to steal, kill, and destroy all that is good, precious, and Christ-like in you and your marriage. (*See John 10:10*) He HATES marriage. He hates full-of-life, God-honoring marriage the most.

Many times, Curtis and I have known the enemy was trying to destroy our marriage and family. Many times, the bad news, disappointments, and challenges have come in waves. They just kept rolling in and pounding the shore of our hearts and spirits. But then Curtis and I started to see the humor in the season, realizing our adversary, the devil, is working overtime on us because he must be very threatened by us.

As we commit to growing together, it will not go unnoticed by your enemy, and it can seem that Winter-like seasons will never end. They can chill us to the core and cause us to question everything. The key to facing attacks and battles is leaning on the One who has power over the situation, your Father in heaven. In these seasons, we need to be ready with more practical ways to walk in God's protection—even in the valley of the shadow of death, as the Psalmist David teaches in one of the most familiar and often-quoted passages:

Psalm 23

¹ The Lord is my shepherd,

I will not be in need.

² He lets me lie down in green pastures;
He leads me beside quiet waters.

³ He restores my soul;

He guides me in the paths of righteousness.

For the sake of His name.

⁴ Even though I walk through the valley of the

shadow of death, I fear no evil, for You are with me;

Your rod and Your staff, they comfort me.

⁵ You prepare a table before me in the presence of my enemies;

You have anointed my head with oil;

My cup overflows.

⁶ Certainly goodness and faithfulness will

follow me all the days of my life,

And my dwelling *will be* in the house of the Lord forever.

It is important to notice that in the first three verses, David is talking *about* God, but when things get desperate—in the shadow of the valley of death—he talks *to* God. And we must learn to do that as well. Turning to God when we are encountering trials and storms exercises our faith. How to respond in crisis situations is to get closer to Him, to look to Him as our provider and protector. We can get lost in the pain of what is happening and talk *about* God. Our response needs to be pause, turn toward God, and talk *to* Him.

Who Am I in Christ?

Building Our Identity and Purpose on Christ

I WENT THROUGH a season in my late thirties when, from my perspective, God was silent. Up until then I had experienced many revelations and words of knowledge. I cried out, "God, why have you stopped speaking to me?" God did answer that cry: "Because you don't DO anything with it. It stops at you." It hit me to the core because I knew I was keeping all of His beautiful words to myself under the guise of busyness. Again, there was silence for many years. (Some of us insist on wandering the desert for many years before we learn to listen—just saying!)

It occurred to me later that God's Word never returns void but accomplishes all that He intends for it to do. (*See Isaiah 55:11.*) It makes sense that God will not waste a breath or hold us accountable for things he knows we cannot yet understand or handle. It would be like entrusting a two-year-old with driving an automobile. What we perceive as God's silence can be an act of mercy awaiting our maturity and faith. God's timing is sometimes hard to understand and trust, but it is always perfect. God truly isn't ever silent. Even in the darkest days of humanity, God has been speaking, cheering us on toward the prize. We, as humans, have a knack for tuning him out.

We are designed to live every word that comes from God. (*See Matthew 4:4*) So how can I be sure I am hearing God's voice and not my own or the enemy's? Let's look at Elijah for some insight.

When the Prophet Elijah needed confirmation that he was hearing God, he did a very human thing: He went and hid in a cave. He waited; finally, a violent storm arose. He knew God was not speaking from the violent wind, nor was he in the earthquake or fire. It was only when a gentle wind passed that he left the cave. He knew he was hearing from God when he heard the gentle breeze. (*See 1 Kings 19:11-13*)

 **FAITH JOURNEY**

Tuning into His Voice

Read 1 Kings 19:9-15

Today you may be feeling like you are fleeing for your life. You may be questioning everything you have ever thought you heard Jesus promise you. You are not alone. Elijah was one of Israel's most fierce prophets; he faced down Jezebel, who had her own grandsons killed to maintain her power. He called down fire from heaven to prove that Israel's God was the one true God, not Baal. (*See 1 Kings 18:16-40.*)

Even with this great success for the Kingdom of God, Elijah doubted and feared. He was worn down from his battles against the idolatress nation. The key to Elijah's greatness: he consistently turned toward God within his struggles.

God does answer us. We need to stop and listen.

WHILE THE BEGINNING of wisdom is fear of the Lord, we can be confident it is God speaking when the peace falls over us beyond our understanding. We know we are hearing God's call when he leads us to green pastures and quiet waters, as the psalm says. (*See Psalm 23*) The storm, earthquake, and fire may rage to get our attention and draw us off course, but God's gentle whisper is what we must tune our hearts to. We cannot leave our safe place for a response to social media or a phone call from a nosey in-law, or even get rocked by a thoughtless comment from someone within the church. When we are earnestly seeking His face, God's voice will bring us deeper into peace. Closer into His protection and sure foundation. We must allow all the other noise to just pass by and wait for His whisper! (A note: the Holy Spirit does show up in a fervor and causes everything to move past our comfort zone.)

It takes time and intention to tune in to what God is saying to us in the harsh and lonely places. The hurt and worry of attending to the demands "du jour," pardon my French, can require all of our strength—and more. That is why Jesus insists that we, his followers, take time out, get recharged, and rest. It is so amazing that God's design and Jesus' example is when things get tough, the Godly rest: A far cry from "When the going gets tough, the tough get going."

It requires times of recalibration and rest for us to usher God's peace into our hearts. We must align our vision with His, taking on a kingdom mindset. When we have God's peace and rest in his provision, then we can accept that the battle is spiritual. Only then can we think clearly (or at least clearer) and be creative.

Finding the quietness of winter requires preparation. When we hear that inclement weather is approaching, we respond by stocking up on supplies and closing off vulnerable areas to safely weather the storm. Just as we do for our external dwellings, we must do for our hearts and minds: have the Word of God securely in our mouth, the protection of prayer, and a united front with our spouse.

 **TRUE NORTH**

Let It Sink In: Stay in the Cave Until You Hear God's Whisper

Like Elijah, you will have times that feel as if you are fleeing for your life. Practicing hearing and listening for God to whisper during moments of ease will help train you to hear Him in your darkness.

Start today. Allow the truth of His Love and concern for you to sink in: He sent Jesus as ransom for your soul so He would have you with Him for all of eternity. Remind yourself that He is with you, especially in these dark situations. You are his wonderful child, and He truly cares about your suffering. He is also a listening Father who longs to hear your cries and complaints.

Something that helps us is to find a song that reminds us to be still and listen. Some of our favorites are: "House of Miracles" by Brandon Lake, "Good, Good Father" by Chris Tomlin, and "I'll Find

You" by Lecrae and Tori Kelly. Turn the music off, then sit quietly and listen to His nudging. We find Sabbath to be a great time to employ this exercise.

Sometimes the Answer Is "Stay Strong"

THE WORLD IS watching how we as Christians respond to the trials and tribulations around us. The Testimony of gracefully trusting in God's plan and praising Him despite our circumstances is the clearest evidence for the Gospel that we can offer. While Curtis and I were youth leaders back in the late 1990s, we witnessed a couple walk their faith in living color. This testimony is not a prescription or goal for most people walking through a desperate hour, but in this one situation God used superhuman strength to send His message. This couple's adopted son, who was quite troubled, shot himself and died. There was no clear evidence if it was intentional or an accident. In a small town, word travels fast, which adds to the hurt.

The tragedy took place just a few weeks before Easter. The father was cast in a role with Curtis and other men in the church depicting the Last Supper. Their first performance was one week after the tragedy. The funeral was one day before, in the same sanctuary. This couple made the decision for him to continue with the play despite the fresh personal pain they were enduring. I will never forget that night. The husband (the boy's father) played his role with passion and integrity, and the wife (the boy's mother) sat in the second row, weeping when the play solicited it. The rest of us, knowing what they were going through, wept quite a bit ourselves.

Over the weeks and months that followed, they continued in fellowship with the congregation. There was so much grace oozing out of them. The boy's parents reached out to us in encouragement for our role as his youth leaders. Curtis and I did our best to help the other members of the youth group deal with the emotions around the tragedy. There was this beautiful acceptance of God's sovereignty despite the very real hurt and confusion. This couple exemplified the servant love most of us talk about. They chose to keep the winter on the outside and not let it sink into their hearts. It strengthened my faith and continues to do so.

Sing Your Song

Play songs for each other that you feel best describe or reflect your marriage. Curtis likes to play "Crazy Girl" (about me) by the Eli Young Band, while I choose "Humble and Kind" by Tim McGraw or "Happy Man" by Jason Eady. Our marriage theme song has been "When I'm Sixty-Four" by the Beatles.

We like to keep playlists on our Spotify. While playing our playlists we often walk down memory lane, or dream and plan for the next fun adventure. There are also tears and prayers of thanksgiving for the strength to continue. If we have a special trip or event coming up, we start collecting and adding songs to a new playlist with that name. For example, we have Dayton, Maui mix, and we will be starting our thirty-fifth anniversary mix soon.

IF YOU AND your spouse decide to do this, your playlist should bring up great memories of happiness but should also include times when you overcame adversity. You will want the songs to compliment your partner and cause joy or peace to bubble up in you both. If you and your spouse don't share a common musical taste, choose songs in the other person's genre—this speaks volumes in the self-sacrifice arena, especially if you do it for each other.

> Two are better than one because they have a good
> return for their labor. For if either of them falls, the
> one will lift up his companion. But woe to the one
> who falls when there is not another to lift him up.
>
> **ECCLESIASTES 4:9-10**

Like following a recipe, getting the right ingredients together before you undertake the cooking can alleviate headaches and disappointments later. We must practice listening and looking to God and His Word before we can hope to be a help to each other. Staying in focus with who our Heavenly Father has made us to be, as well as to His truth He speaks to us and over us, we will avoid pitfalls that so easily ensnare us.

Ingredients—Falling from Grace

Biblical Couple: David and the Wife of Uriah (Bathsheba)

THINK OF OUR precious David: the shepherd who killed the lion and the bear while tending sheep. The warrior who faced and brought down Goliath with a sling and a stone. The psalmist. The king who slew thousands in the name of the Lord, and the man chosen to free Israel. The one of whom God spoke: "He is a man after my own heart." (*See Acts 13:22*) Could this be the same David who had his close friend murdered to cover up his infidelity with that friend's wife? One and the same!

The story reads like an episode of a current reality TV show. David should have been with his men out on the battlefield. Instead, he is taking a little R&R roaming around the castle and finds himself longing for another man's wife. Uriah is one of his "mighty men" and has risked his own life several times for David, but this friendship does not stand in the way of a bored king who, at this point, is enjoying the spoils of his position to the extent he stops putting God's Word as his highest priority. After sleeping with this bathing beauty, Bathsheba, he tries to cover up her pregnancy by having Uriah sent back from battle. But the plan is foiled when Uriah's honor to the king and the nation of Israel will not allow him to go home to his wife until the battle is over. Finding himself at risk of being exposed, David takes his deceit to the next level. He orders Uriah to go unaided to the heat of the battle, where he will meet certain death. (*See Samuel 11*)

After Uriah's murder, David takes Bathsheba as his wife. God brings swift justice to Uriah's name, and the child dies shortly after birth. David repents and is forgiven for his sin. But the consequences of his betrayal are severe. 2 Samuel 12:15-20 records how bitter the pain of the loss is. Perhaps David rightly blames himself during his time of mourning. His guilt causes him much anguish. After David realizes that nothing, he does will change God's mind, he accepts the verdict and goes back to his duties as king. God grants David and Bathsheba another son, who will become the successor to his father, Solomon. He will become known as the wisest man who ever lived. He will build the temple that God has not allowed David to build.

God restores David's lineage, and He does it in a mighty way. Until Jesus appears, David continues to be lifted up as the standard of a "Man after God's own Heart." Several times in the Old Testament, after his fall, God says, "My servant David." If we have sinned, we need to take it to God, humbly asking for forgiveness and grace. We will find that God our Father is the God of second chances. He can still use us for His good purposes here on earth. For example, after David's fall from grace, he wrote several psalms, which are wonderful reflections of God's willingness and desire to forgive and restore us.

 **FAITH JOURNEY**

Keeping Track of God's Grace and Forgiveness

Read the following psalms David wrote after his great fall in his affair with Bathsheba. Write down any sin that is still causing you guilt. As you read these verses, notice David's confidence in God's forgiveness and His continuing protection.

Psalm 32: Blessedness of Forgiveness and of Trust in God (verse 8: God makes a promise to David)

Psalm 51: A Contrite Sinner's Prayer (verse 10: only God can bring us into holiness)

Psalm 86: Supplication and Trust (verse 3: David reflects on and trusts in God's character)

Psalm 122: Prayer for Peace of Jerusalem (verse 1: "Let us go to the house of the Lord")

WHILE MOST OF us have not murdered a close friend to cover up infidelity with their spouse, many of us have wrestled under guilt that we had any part to play in a bitter season we experienced. It is good to have a conscience and grieve for our part in disobeying God's loving instructions. However, we must be able to accept the forgiveness that Jesus' sacrifice brings and get back to the business of honoring God.

Some winters bring guilt, self-doubt, and blame. These battles of the mind and heart remind us how much we need grace. We should also take the opportunity to extend grace as well. Others' suffering within the season is also raw and susceptible to further hurt during trials and storms. It is good to take our deep pain and complaints to God in prayer before making too many actions while we are in a suffering season.

What we learn from David's mistakes: Everyone is capable of falling hard. If we take our eye off of the calling God has given us, allowing our eyes to wander to what others have, we risk coveting their blessings. We will save ourselves many heartaches if we focus on what God has done for us and what He has promised to do. Falling into the trap of comparison on social media or trying to keep up with the Joneses or our friend group can lead us into an ungrateful heart. God restored David's heart and mind, but the consequence of sin that followed David's family was great. Sin will leave a stain in our lives unless we allow God, through the forgiveness of Jesus and the working of the Holy Spirit, to cleanse and change us, from the inside out.

May 24, 1976, Terri's Cookbook

Soup of Frog legs

Take 2 dozen frogs' legs and pour over them lukewarm water let them remain in; about 5 minutes, but not to cook. Pour off the water and add equal quantities of milk and water sufficient to cover, cook moderately about half an hour, simmer a small onion, chopped, in butter, add to soup with a quart of rich milk, 2 tablespoonfuls butter, a little salt and pepper and a dessertspoonful of chopped parsley, skim the legs from the soup and remove them, in the bones, put the meat into the tureen with a tablespoonful thick cream, and a little celery, apple, celery, the soup with this, and serve at once

Apparently, I was a foodie way before it was "a thing." Back in elementary school, we created cookbooks of our favorite recipes, a few noteworthy entries being oyster stew, fried eel, baked white fish, and even squirrel soup . . . So, this is not my first book to be published, though I feel like this present work is a little more palatable.

Smooth Seas Never a Skilled Sailor Made

"On that day, when evening came, He said to them, 'Let's go over to the other side.' After dismissing the crowd, they took Him along with them in the boat, just as He was; and other boats were with Him. And a fierce gale of wind developed, and the waves were breaking over the boat so much that the boat was already filling with water. And yet Jesus Himself was in the stern, asleep on the cushion; and they woke Him and said to Him, 'Teacher, do You not care that we are perishing?' And He got up and rebuked the wind and said to the sea, 'Hush, be still.' And the wind died down and it became perfectly calm. And He said to them, 'Why are you afraid? Do you still have no faith?'" (Mark 4:35-40)

We notice that Jesus gave a command: "Let's go over to the other side." When Jesus calls us to do something in His name, He will see it through. Once the storm arises, the disciples could have reflected on the statement Jesus made about going to the other side. Instead, they focus on the storm, wake him, and begin to accuse him of not caring about them. (I can certainly relate. When life sifts and shakes me, I often panic and pray frantically about my situation and start blaming God and accusing him of apathy toward me.) After Jesus calms the storm, which was very real, he rebukes his disciples for being afraid and without faith. Seeing myself in this story, I have come to realize that standing in the right posture when the storms rage in my life is faith in action. What if, instead of waking Jesus, the disciples had lain down on the pillow beside him? What if, when the very real and heartbreaking circumstances arise in our lives, we lay down on the pillow beside Jesus, believing that he has called us to "go over to the other side"?

Let's take our marriages to that depth. To quote a dear friend, "If you can't be tested, you can't be trusted." The storms are the training ground by which our skills are sharpened.

When the world witnesses how we love each other even in our pain and darkness, they will know we are His disciples. When you are living a Honeymoon Life of joy, intimacy, and passion, the world will be attracted to it and ask: What is your secret? "We were told to get to the other side!" will be our response.

WORK IT OUT TOGETHER

Approaching Grace

Think back to a storm that you have faced recently. It can be small, like a temporary financial struggle, or a large, long-term challenge like a job loss. It may be helpful for each spouse to do this individually and then share collectively.

During this struggle, how did you approach the throne of grace? Did you come as a child to their father, expecting love and mercy? Did you know that God would use this situation in your life to draw you closer to him? Did you act in confidence to "get to the other side"?

Make a list of the biggest struggles you have overcome in your marriage up until today. Include as much information and specifics. If you have beginning and ending dates, those are powerful.

Now, make a list of promises or struggles that remain unresolved. Begin to pray as a trusting child over these situations, going back to the list of victories you made. Thank God and remind Him that you are very confident in His character and that He is your good Father.

A small journal can be very useful. Curtis loves making lists on his phone. Keep this as a continuous prayer journal and add it to your calendar.

Living the Honeymoon Life

One of the best habits Curtis and I have established is a daily reading of God's Word together. One morning, we had a precious encounter together while simply honoring our commitment. The lesson that day quoted Cory Ten Boom: "Never hold onto anything so tightly that Jesus can't take it from you." The question was then proposed, "What are you holding onto that Jesus can't take from you?" We each identified things that we keep from Jesus. We laughed and prayed and resolved to release 100 percent, to surrender all, to Jesus. This was a preparation moment for us. It helped us secure our Spiritual Armor. Being consistently fitted with the equipment of heaven, your marriage can thrive, even in the winter.

Lying on the Pillow

I AM ATTEMPTING to practice this habit as difficulties arise. I am not there yet, but I have found some growth in this area. For instance, on Father's Day, one of our daughters left our house and went off the grid, leaving us worried and wondering about her well-being instead of being together with Curtis and the rest of the family. We have her location shared on our phones, but knowing where a phone is does not always yield confidence that the loved one is all right. (She may not have her phone with her.) After many hours, beginning in the early morning, we finally heard from her. She texted her father, "I'm not dead." I lost it—I blew a gasket! After hours of being concerned, I found her quip upsetting and her attitude dismissive. I had a quick call with her where I was less than gracious! She had promised to come back to the house soon. In the meantime, God showed me that I needed to rest in Him. I needed to lie down and concentrate on Philippians 4:8: "Whatever is true, whatever is honorable, whatever is right, whatever is pure, whatever is lovely, whatever is commendable, if there is any excellence and if anything, worthy of praise, dwell on these things."

It was not easy. It did not come naturally. Since I had enlisted this habit before, I started with what I had practiced, God's word is true. Being a child of the Most High God is honorable. It is right to extend the grace I have been given. It is pure to love my children unconditionally. It is lovely to hold my daughters in high esteem and to want the best for them. A good report of my child, whom I thought was injured or worse, had been given. It is excellent that I have the opportunity to speak Christ into her another day. God's mercy in bringing her back to us is proof that He will work all of things for His glory and is worthy of praise! I added, Lord, please humble this child before she returns here, and allow the healing to be quick and complete and let us get on with celebrating my amazing husband and awesome father today.

When she first arrived, I stayed in my room, keeping silent in my bed. I waited a couple of hours before I approached her. When I did, she immediately apologized and humbly asked to assist with Father's Day preparations. God had answered my mother's cry, not just for the physical safety but for the forward spiritual and mental progress of our daughter. It was truly a miracle. But God is romantic that way.

Recipe for a Strong Marriage

Our family favorite, "Nana Noodles," is handmade egg noodles cooked in turkey broth. My mom's version was born from watching her mom make them during Christmas when my mom was a child. Her mom made the noodles first and then dried them. My mom asked her, "Why do you dry the noodles when you are going to put them in liquid and rehydrate them?" Gramma responded, "Because my mom dried them." Nana experimented with the recipe without drying the noodles and discovered the texture was much better without drying. Sometimes you just have to ask, there could be a better way to do it.

There is an art of making these noodles turn out like Nana's. Nana Noodles require attention as they cook, and there is no ignoring them. If they are stirred too much, they are tough and chewy. If you drop them in all at once, they will stick together, and you will end up with one ball of uncooked mess. If you don't stir often, they will stick to the bottom. If you don't monitor the liquid and add as needed, they will not become tender.

For all this effort they are so worth it! There is nothing as comforting as Nana Noodles served over mashed potatoes. It is like a hug inside your belly. It's a symbol of the warmth and comfort of gathering around the table with family during the holidays. Even as the weather stirs its bitter breath, we are warm, safe, and well-fed in our loving home. This much-anticipated dish at our holiday gatherings is always the star of the meal, but the true reward is the time spent together.

My role in holiday dinners is not too much in the noodle-making. My ability to cut noodles or potatoes with any consistency is poor at best. When I cut noodles, they end up as all shapes and sizes.

Fortunately, I have four children and a husband who are all very gifted in the area of homogeneous dicing, so they get that assignment. Curtis is also frequently called on to mash the potatoes—after they are perfectly diced and cooked.

Living the Honeymoon Life

In a well-balanced arrangement, everyone lends a hand in the preparation. Much of the memory-making comes from the time spent together in the kitchen as much as the eating around the table. Men, you play a huge role in setting the tone for peace and joy for everyone during these large gatherings.

Perhaps you guide smaller children in helping set the table. Perhaps you mash the potatoes. Of course, the carving of the turkey or ham is a very manly role to play. Everyone who can be trusted can bring food to the table, and everyone should be a part of the clean-up. Having a plan that blesses both you and your spouse for how everyone is involved in the process makes for a smoother and more enjoyable holiday memory.

Nana (Judi) getting some "help" from her great-grandchild,
Rory, while making the famous Nana Noodles

Nana Noodles

Part I: Cooking the Turkey

1. Wash and season the skin and the cavity of the turkey with onion powder and lemon pepper.

2. Place the turkey in a stock pot big enough to accommodate and completely cover the bird.

3. Add water, about two cups to start at the bottom of the stock pot.

4. Cover and bake turkey until internal temperatures reaches 165 degrees.

(*To calculate the time needed, estimate 13-15 minutes per pound.)

Part II: Making the Noodles

While turkey is cooking, make the noodles. Combine:

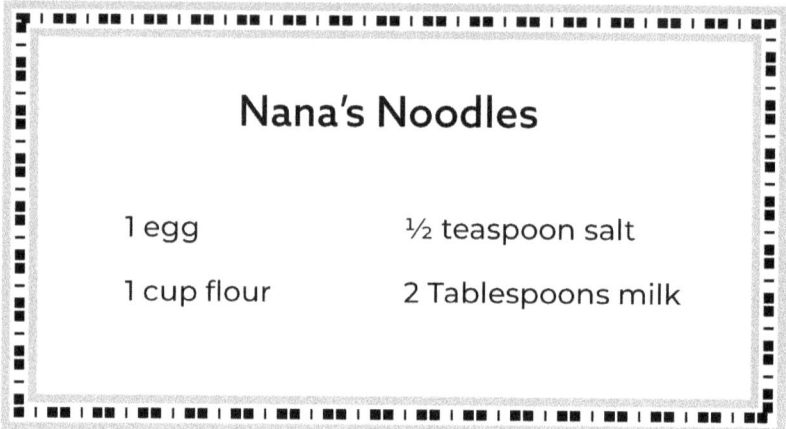

Nana's Noodles

1 egg   ½ teaspoon salt

1 cup flour   2 Tablespoons milk

(Adjust the recipe to fit your needs. The number of servings you want will determine how many eggs to use. For a full family dinner, I use a 3-egg batch, multiplying all ingredients by 3.)

1. In a small cup or bowl, combine eggs and milk, mix.

2. In a large mixing bowl, combine flour and salt, mix.

3. Make a well in the flour, add wet ingredients, combine to make a dough. If the dough is too crumbly and will not form a ball, add two Tablespoons of milk and combine, continue until dough forms a smooth ball in your hands.

4. Roll noodles out with a floured rolling pin on a floured surface to prevent sticking. Dough should be about ¼ inch thick when finished. Cut long strips about 4 inches wide. Stack strips, adding more flour as necessary. Cut noodles off of strips about ¼ inch wide, flicking noodles off the knife into a pile. Using your floured hands, gently lift noodles to separate, adding flour as needed.

5. Remove turkey from the pot, leaving the broth and drippings.

6. Put the stock pot on the stovetop. Add water to the turkey broth to measure about 4 quarts. Add salt, pepper, and chicken bouillon to taste. Be careful not to over-salt; the bullion adds salt. Add a dash of yellow food color.

7. Stirring frequently, bring broth to a low rolling boil.

8. Once a consistent boil has been reached, while stirring constantly, begin dropping noodles by hand, separating them as they drop into the water. We generally make this a two-person step; one person stirs and the other drops the noodles. YOU CANNOT RUSH THIS STEP. Once all noodles have been added, continue stirring until the pot returns to a low boil. At this point you will know if you need to add more water. Add enough water to ensure noodles have space to boil and move around separately. Once you are confident the noodles are cooking and not sticking (typically about a 20- to 30-minute step) lightly cover and simmer, stirring every 10 to 15 minutes. Test noodles after about 30 to 45 minutes.

9. Once noodles are tender, turn off the heat and stir. In our family, when serving, we each add the desired amount of turkey onto our noodles and serve it over mashed potatoes. Please enjoy responsibly—they are that good!

Preparation Before the Frost

AS A CHILD, I knew the reality of getting ready for winter. It meant the final harvesting, canning, and tilling of the garden, before the first frost ushered winter weather in. We would insulate our old windows by covering them with plastic, keeping the cold out and the heat in. There was weather-stripping to place around doors, and once the deep freeze moved in, we would plug in the car batteries to ensure that they would start the next morning. We did not have a garage in my younger years, and my mom's car got priority under the carport. (Our carport was an extension of the roof over the driveway that came all the way up to the house to keep the elements off that area.) My dad, however, was not so pampered. I remember watching him get layered up in his thermal coat, boots, gloves, and hat, then braving the snow, heading out to his unsheltered car, starting it up, and allowing it to warm up and defrost so he could scrape the windows.

The winters were bitter and long. On the inside looking out, warm in my cozy pajamas, I was comfy and safe seeing him do this. I was well aware that if I wanted to step out the door, I would need to don the proper protection.

In a season of ease, it is difficult to appreciate how vital our winter apparel will be when we need it. Preparing to face bitter challenges, especially as a couple, requires some outfitting. What we have stored away in the summer would now need to be brought out to use. Think "Holy North Face." Our spiritual protection, as detailed in Ephesians 6, requires us to practice utilizing each piece of Spiritual Armor: faith, truth, righteousness, salvation, sword of the Spirit, and the Gospel of Peace. It is what we do before troubles arise that prepares us to face difficulties. Curtis and I have been challenged with some extremely difficult moments in our relationship over almost four decades. It is the protection we have received from our Heavenly Father and our well-fitted Spiritual Armor that has gotten us through. We live by the motto we learned in the Air Force and Martial Arts: "As you train, you will fight!"

Some challenges came on suddenly, like an early frost. Like the moment we got a call that one of our children was being admitted to the hospital from school. Many we saw coming and had time to prepare for: My father's passing was several years in the making. Whether it's a shock or something foreseen, getting through these seasons of winter-like events demands mindfulness.

Taking Action

Curtis and I experienced a very difficult season in our 24th year of marriage. We had three teenagers in the home, and it proved to be a great struggle. I was feeling like a complete failure. We had done parenting to the best of our ability, and for the majority of their childhoods, we had harmony and unity within the family. I stayed home with the children when they were little, and even after they entered school, I worked around their schedules to be an involved mom. But it had not given us the result we'd expected or thought we deserved. We were riddled with rebellion, disobedience, and contempt for everything we had taught them and stood for. We had visits to jail, mental hospitals, hospitals, Child Protective Services, probation, and courtrooms. I cried out in desperation one day. We were on a walk and exasperated, and I said to Curtis, "I have an exit strategy if you want to come with me!"

Curtis heard my heart cry and stepped up: He sent me a spreadsheet. (Don't be jealous; he's a real romantic like that.) It was his way to offer and organize a long overdue honeymoon. I needed a break, and he responded. He did extensive research and sent me several choices to consider in the Caribbean. We settled on Jost Van Dyke. This destination is not for everyone. This tiny island with two hundred full-time residents does not offer all-inclusive options. It is a "carry-in all of your supplies from Tortola" spot. But for us it was perfect.

CURTIS' INPUT

Paying Attention

It is easy for me as the breadwinner to get distracted by work. Sometimes it is a great relief to go to work when there are difficulties at home. But when the wife of my youth was completely spent, that reflected on me. I was the one who had let it get that hopeless. I needed to step into action quickly. I had to be at my best. God guided me, and ultimately both of us, to the complete relaxation reset we needed.

WE RENTED A bungalow on a seven-home property but ended up being the only occupants for the entire two weeks. This meant we had a private cove beach. It was like being shipwrecked on Gilligan's Island! Curtis and I soaked in all the rest and relaxation and peace and quiet. It was an absolute reset. Even though there were still issues to be managed back home, there was never again a feeling of desperation or that the season would never end. And I stopped listening to the lie that "I was a failure." We have a perfect Father in Heaven and all of His children except one (Jesus) have rebelled, so I am in good company.

You don't have to hit a hard reset like we did to bring about the positive effect of a sabbatical. Taking a lovely drive together near your home or getting a nice lunch can offer a huge dose of peace of mind and communion for your marriage. A date night with a quiet supper and dessert at home, just the two of you, can be a great rejuvenation.

The Secret Sauce: Preparing for Inclement Weather

Whether you are facing a job loss, health issues, the loss of a family member, financial stress, or a troubled child, these arduous seasons happen to everyone. Jesus modeled how to respond to extreme pressure in the Garden of Gethsemane. Though He was fully man and fully God, He still suffered under the weight of His circumstances. Knowing what He would endure over the next few days, He was crushed under the weight of pain and anguish. So, He prayed! Fervently and raw in the sight of God alone. If Jesus needed to stop and pray in His hour of distress, how much more do we? We cannot push through heartbreaks and trials as if everything is normal. Like Jesus, we need to go fervently to prayer when the darkness falls.

 **FAITH JOURNEY**

Who's Got Your Back

Read Matthew 26:36-46

Jesus was abandoned before the arrest in the Garden. His followers could not stay awake to pray with Him. In your darkest hours, you may feel alone, but God has got your back. He provided armor for the rest of you!

Therefore, take up the full armor of God, so that you will be able to resist on the evil day, and having done everything, to stand firm. Stand firm therefore, having belted your waist with truth, and having put on the breastplate of righteousness, and having strapped on your feet the preparation of the gospel of peace; in addition to all, taking up the shield of faith with which you will be able to extinguish all the flaming arrows of the evil one. And take the helmet of salvation and the sword of the Spirit, which is the Word of God.

EPHESIANS 6:13-17

TAKE TIME TO COLOR

Living the Honeymoon Life

There is an ancient military formation that I think could use reviving: a "shield wall."

To defend against flanking attacks or to withstand a heavy attack, soldiers would form a shield wall, gathering in a tight circle and placing their shields in front of them. Shields would overlap to create an impenetrable barrier. Offense could still be effective from within the encapsulated hoard, through archers or even swordplay. The idea was to create a safe space to retreat while the battle raged.

Today, while defending within the Winter season, we must lock shields and create these safe spaces. This will allow us to answer our spouses' and families' needs during the battle. We can help each other don the armor. For example, if I am struggling with faith, Curtis comes along and prays powerful prayers, out loud, as declarations. I know that I am completely covered in protection. Likewise, if he is struggling with the confidence to move into a new area God is calling him into, I speak out loud and declare his appointment and assignment to that seat. He is then free to step out in boldness, protected by my love and honor.

We are meant to cleave together during the hardest, darkest moments, to get cozy within the battle and cover each other's weaknesses in our faith.

The Right Fit for a Warrior's Mindset

ONE OF THE most critical pieces of armor during a formidable season is the Helmet of Salvation. But what are the practical applications of the spiritual armor—specifically, the helmet? The concept is not foreign, but can we appreciate that the inside of our head needs protection as well?

Science has shown in numerous studies that prolonged negative thinking causes degenerative brain diseases, cardiovascular problems, and digestive issues, according to Bree Maloney with Marque Medical. [11]People who are pessimistic also recover much slower from sicknesses. How can negative thoughts affect our spiritual well-being?

If we entertain negative thoughts, it does not take long for them to take root, causing us to hone in on all our spouse's flaws. When I am busy focusing on how my husband is not the man he should be, I miss the opportunity to celebrate and help him step into the man that he already is—which is a pretty awesome man!

If we are to be Christ-like, especially in our marriages, there is a high bar on how we think of our spouse and subsequently how we treat them. Having Christ's grace and love for our spouse causes us to have servant love for them. We begin to watch for opportunities to out-serve each other. Commit today to turning your negative thoughts away, using the salvation that Jesus gained for you on the Cross. It is the first place to win the battle.

Find Purpose Through Pain

Our ways are not God's ways. (*See Isaiah 55:9*) It is so painful and difficult to see someone suffering when we know that God can do something about it. Why aren't all requests answered "yes"?

The Bible teaches that the heart of God is a good Father. We have seen his loving kindness in the Bible and in our lives and creation. We are promised that He hears us when we cry out to Him. And yet, God is not a genie in a bottle that grants our every wish. He has omniscience to see what we cannot.

During his ministry on earth, Jesus healed many, but he also left some unanswered. We don't have the secret formula of why this is true. But when he did perform physical healings here on earth, he reminded us that it was merely a sign to point people to the love of God. But he warned us that it an "evil and adulterous generation seeks after a sign; a sign will not be given, except the sign of Jonah." (Matthew 16:4) If the sign, the miracle, is our end purpose, then perhaps our hearts are misguided. But if we are looking for God to be glorified by the miracle, then we have the mind of Christ.

God is a perfect Father, so we can anticipate His great mercy and love to show up. We look to Him for complete and total transformation of our trials. That is not evil. But if His answer, which is often the case, is different than what we expect, we must rest knowing His character is always good.

You Can't Always Get What You Want!

But when Jesus heard *this*, He said, 'This sickness is not meant for death, but *is* for the glory of God, so that the Son of God may be glorified by it.' Now Jesus loved Martha and her sister, and Lazarus. Yet, when He heard that he was sick, He then stayed two days *longer* in the place where He was. Then after this, He said to the disciples, 'Let's go to Judea again.'

JOHN 11:4-7

As we look at Jesus' final days on earth, we see God's heart for the broken and hurting. Jesus' friend Lazurus became very ill. The sisters of Lazarus, Mary and Martha, reach out to Jesus, knowing He could have healed their brother. If only He had been there, they knew Lazarus would have been saved. But Jesus waited. He allowed Lazarus to die, before responding to the request for Him to intervene. Jesus loves to say yes to healing our heartbreaks. He suffered on the cross, died, and was resurrected to defeat every letter of the curse that we live under. Still, it can often surprise us how and when He brings the answer to light.

Our part is to point others to God in the sign of the miracle, so they can see He is still the good Father that Jesus modeled. Our Winters can bring testimonies of power, love, and faithfulness out of the darkness. But like Nana Noodles on simmer, the timing and temperature are critical for a good finish. We must allow the flavor of the Holy Spirit's presence to soak through our toughness. We must be in a state of allowing it to soften us, not harden us. Trusting that God has our best interest in His plan can make the simmering process more tolerable. We cannot know at the moment what the entirety of God's purpose is for His answer, but we can be sure He has good plans for us!

 FUN & GAMES

Face to Face

Nana Noodles must simmer after they have been lovingly mixed. This is a perfect time to play a game to ease the waiting period.

Some of our favorites for long, quiet evenings have been Backgammon and Abalone. Both are two-person strategy games. Backgammon involves a board that is set up with checkers. Two dice are rolled to determine the movement count, and strategy is dependent on your opponent's piece positions. The object is to get all of your checkers home without being caught and sent back by your opponent. The first player with all checkers safely home wins!

Abalone is a game of marbles on a tray. They can be pushed in sets of three or fewer; however, you can only push your opponent when your count outnumbers theirs. The player who pushes all of the opponent's marbles off wins!

WINTER

Fresh Starts and Do-Overs

Becoming Master Musicians

ONE OF THE biggest misconceptions that our society perpetuates is the "happily ever after." We are sold this image from our very youngest exposures with stories like Cinderella and Prince Charming, Snow White, or any Hallmark movie. Country music is filled with the boy getting the truck, so the girl jumps up in the "shotgun seat,oh," (from "This Is How We Roll," by Florida Georgia Line). Every genre of music and art has its part to play in extending the concept of the idyllic magical wedding being the end of the relationship story.

I like to say that love songs are to true romance and intimacy what reality TV is to reality. They don't give the proper expectations for living real life. Instead of experiencing wine and roses every day, we are faced with dirty dishes and laundry. Maintenance of life should not squelch our joy in the journey; it is a part of the learning to love like Jesus. Instead, we should focus our efforts on making our marriages into "reality love songs." The verses go more like this: "You lost your job. We need to pay the rent, and the kids need shoes, but we still fight this good fight together! Hand in hand!"

All good stories and music have moments of conflict or tension. It would not be a movie worth watching, a book worth reading, or a song worth listening to if there were no crescendo. Think "elevator music."

Confession: I watch an occasional Hallmark movie. I am always amazed that with one repeating storyline, this genre still sells. How many movies can there be with: boy meets girl under false pretenses, they can't stand each other, one or both of them are about to get married, then BLAMO, they fall in love!? Still, no matter how many movies Hallmark cranks out, there is a very devoted following. Why? Because we relate to and long for a hero to come along and prove that good does triumph over evil.

The same is true in a page-turning book or great pieces of music that also rend our hearts and cause us grief for a short while; then, the crescendo ends and we can rest easy because order is restored. To have our marriages play like a "reality love song," we must practice being master musicians.

First, we must practice "tuning up." We will do this by working on our personal value and worth in Christ, our identity of being a child of God. We are co-heirs in Christ Jesus; we must live by the spirit in the knowledge of the truth. Practicing our child of God status is step one.

Step two is all about keeping tempo and playing in the same key with our mate. Keeping our hearts and minds protected in agreement with our spouse. No matter how well each member of an orchestra might play their own part, if there is not a collective key and tempo, the result is just noise. Staying in unison requires both spouses to seek the other's good and the glory of God above all else.

Step three is playing the music you've been given. When the situations arise in your marriage, you don't quit. The struggle of these moments is not the theme of the song; it is the conflict that needs to be overcome. It is a strengthening lesson. Though it is uncomfortable, it can bring about growth and fitness for the journey.

To ensure that your marriage and your life don't stop at the inevitable crescendo, you will need to continue to work on the daily principles and applications of leaning into God by staying in His Word and in prayer. We must keep practicing! Trust in what He has laid out in your path, and in His design of your marriage. Remember, these bumps and conflicts make us stronger and are part of the entirety of your story.

The Great Mystery—One Flesh

WE ARE CALLED to be not just unified in all circumstances but to truly become one flesh. Picture an orchestra performing. Each member plays their own part, but together they make one song. This cannot be accomplished or even fully understood in our humanness, so it must come from our time with the Father.

"This mystery is great; but I am speaking with reference to Christ and the church. Nevertheless, each individual among you also is to love his own wife even as himself, and the wife must see to it that she respects her husband." (Ephesians 5:32-33)

Paul refers to the "mystery" in comparison to Christ and His Bride, the Church. There is no closer glimpse of what eternity will be like than the covenant of marriage here on earth. Your marriage was blessed by God to carry His covenant to the world. It must be shining and resplendent. When we respond to crisis and pain in love and grace, we become a beautiful example for other marriages to follow.

Read the accounts of the couples from the Bible. There is only one perfect marriage, the one between Jesus Christ and his Bride, the Church. We are to be guide markers, pointing the way to Jesus' model of marriage. Our response to setbacks and struggles will shine the light on God's strength working within us, modeling the servant love of Jesus.

 **WORK IT OUT TOGETHER**

Comparisons

Take time to answer questions independently. When you have your answers, put them in the Venn diagrams on the next page to visually see where you overlap.

How can I better practice living in my identity as God's Child?

HIS _____

HERS_____

OURS _____

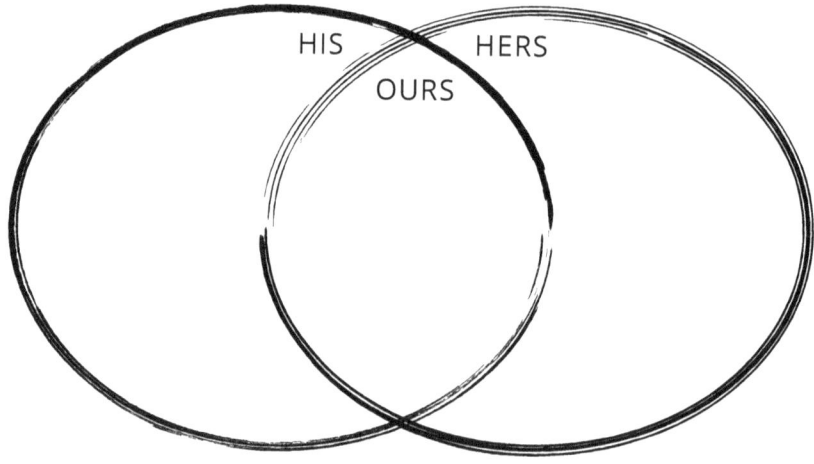

How can I focus on my spouse as God's child?

HIS_____

HERS_____

OURS _____

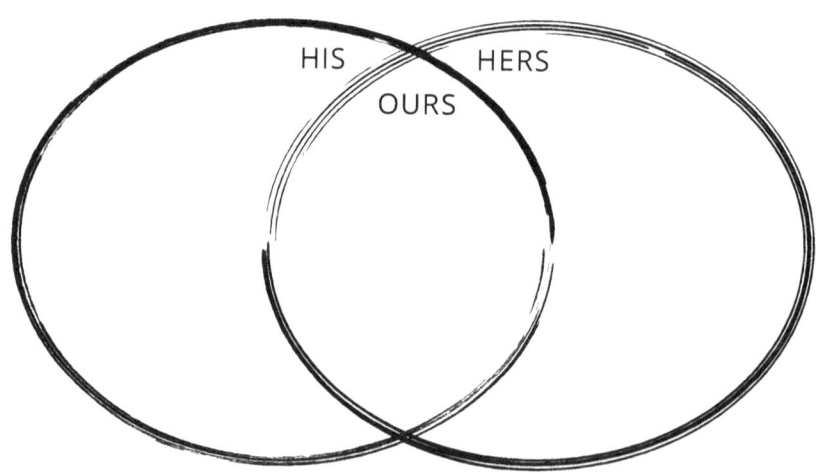

In what areas of our marriage do we get hung up?

HIS _____

HERS _____

OURS _____

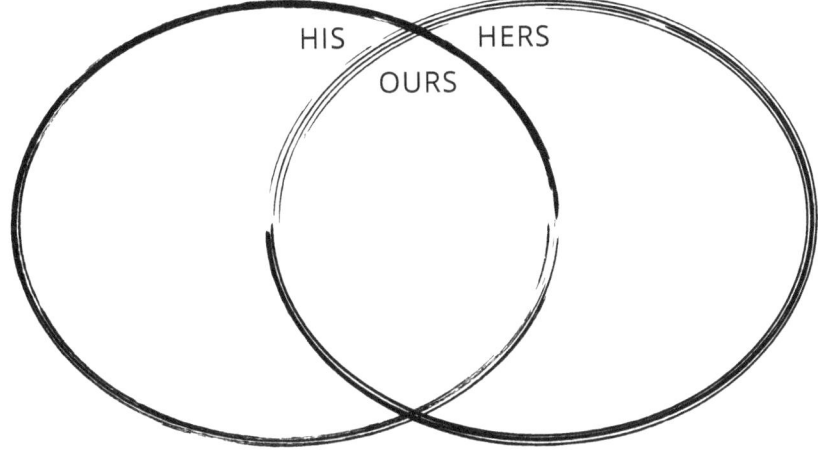

What Bible verse do I stand on when life gets tough?

HIS _____

HERS _____

OURS _____

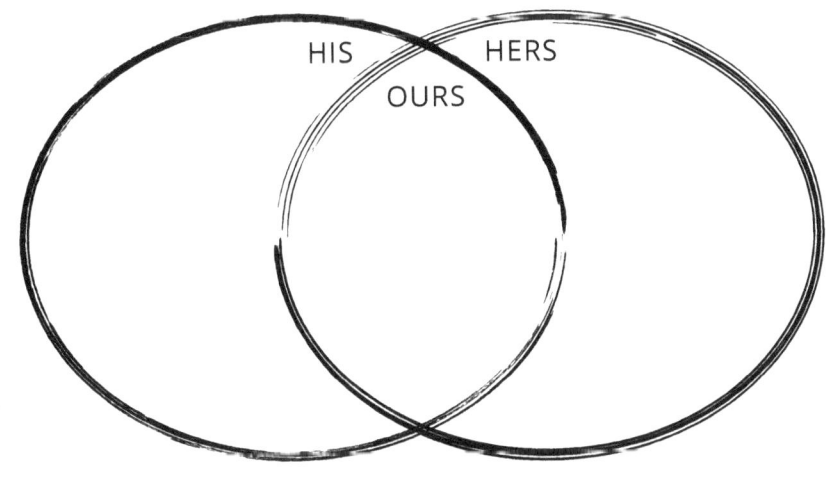

Keeping Unity While Allowing for Individuality

While we are being beaten against the rocks by the storms of life, it is so easy to start to view our partners as the enemy. It can feel like we are being pulled in opposite directions. Each of us will need to process the grief and stress of the bitter season as our individual personalities require, allowing each partner to travel the road of healing at their own pace. We may get down the road a bit, then suffer a setback. Be patient with the process and the potholes. Give your spouse the space and grace to journey the grief path as they need, without taking it personally.

There may be instances within the journey where your spouse might need your loving insight. They might be wallowing instead of processing. (These moments may require professional intervention. Don't be afraid to ask for help. Jesus did not carry His cross all the way up to Golgotha alone. We all have moments where we cannot bear the weight without assistance.) Ask permission to speak into their dark space without judging or applying your own opinions on their grief. You are to sharpen each other, not grind each other to a pulp!

SALT AND LIGHT

Keeping It in Perspective

When our children were little, I would take them on field trips. I would often get off course and end up on the scenic route. Realizing it, the kids would shout from the back of the minivan, "Mom, are we lost again?" To which I would reply, "No, we are just checking what other ways we might get there." We would all laugh, and if the diversion took us too far off course the kids would get ice cream or "shave ice" for their patience, and for not telling dad.

Curtis' response: "I never knew this." I guess these kids did good then!

Krupp Marriage Experience

How Did We Respond When We Experienced Deep Wounds?

HONESTLY, WHEN WE faced a great hurt within the body, our church, we pulled back. While the community should have been our best defense partners, we found ourselves hiding out to avoid exposure. We were so overwhelmed by the intensity of the rebellion and tired from the battle that we chose not to put ourselves out into a larger community for a time. It was the wrong decision.

When the church we had attended religiously for five years lost its youth leaders to another opportunity, a couple of men from the congregation stepped in to lead temporarily. But they were not trained nor fit to lead in the image of Christ, and word came to us through our children that there were deep issues. Our children began to dislike and distrust corporate fellowship. It came to a head, and we suddenly stopped attending this church. Subsequently, no one called or reached out in an attempt to understand or help. Community needs to flow both ways. The wounded must be surrounded; the strong need to offer protection, not judgment. It will be everyone's turn at some point to receive and a time to give.

When building your community, don't be afraid to test-drive different churches, small groups, and circles. You are not marrying a church. You are there for the time and season while God needs you to serve there. This is different from church hopping because things don't go your way.

While Jesus walked the earth and led His church of disciples, there were issues. There is no perfect congregation because there are people there. Don't tolerate a body that is acting contrary to the Word of God, but remember we are all human and make mistakes. Use Godly discernment and allow His Spirit to tell you when it is time to move. Until then, stay where you are.

Likewise, we are not bound by our family history to determine our marriage legacy. We don't have to stick to the friends we made in high school for advice or your coworkers' opinions at the water cooler to build our beliefs. Remember, the disciples abandoned their former lives to follow Jesus; we too must leave behind any encumbrance that keeps us from total commitment to Jesus. You and your spouse are responsible to use your God-given wisdom to seek out and build the proper inner circle, one that will sharpen and protect you in your time of weakness and need. I know of too many horror stories of well-meaning busybodies showing up at hospital rooms and funeral homes to "pray" or give advice to the grieving families. It is our job as the leaders of our families to guard their spiritual well-being against those who would come in as wolves in sheep's clothing. (*See Matthew 7:15*) Choose wisely; Jesus showed us how.

In Mark 8 and Matthew 16, we learn the importance of Jesus' inner circle. Peter just received insight from the Holy Spirit of who Jesus was: "You are the Christ, the Son of the living God." (Matthew 16:16) He was riding high and had just received his new name, "The Rock." He was given the name Simon by his parents, but Jesus speaks into his divine identity as a foundational part of building a new church. But immediately following this glorious moment, the old Simon rears his ugly head, and the old man starts rebuking Jesus. "And *yet* Peter took Him aside and began to rebuke Him, saying, 'God forbid it, Lord! This shall never happen to you!" But He turned and said to Peter, "Get behind Me, Satan! You are a stumbling block to Me; for you are not setting your mind on God's interests, but man's.'" (Matthew 16:22-23)

Jesus as a perfect leader had imperfect followers. They were flawed and self-centered, competitive and self-seeking. They were a bunch of sinners in need of grace, as we all are. We do not advocate for finding a circle full of perfect people; you will never find that. We advocate for finding a circle that "perfectly" helps you grow into the best version of you that you can be on this side of heaven.

WORK IT OUT TOGETHER

Reflections

Take a moment to celebrate a victory you as a couple have already overcome. If God brought you through that adversity, surely, He will bring you through the next one. It is important to thank Him for the work He has already done.

	HIS	HERS	OURS
Remembering the greatest challenge we have overcome together so far			
What we did well during that season			
What we want to do better next winter			

No Room at the Inn

WHEN JESUS CAME to earth the first time, He came as a vulnerable baby. He was not greeted with great fanfare or a royal procession. No. Instead, He was wrapped in rags and laid in an animal's feeding trough. The city of Bethlehem was in the throes of a census, where all people were required to return to the towns of their family lineage to be counted. The sojourners were distracted by the census and competing for basic necessities. There was no time or desire to stop and admire the Messiah, the Savior of the World.

We need to save room for our Savior in our hearts, especially during the Winter seasons of our lives, allowing the "Good News" to sink into our hearts and souls and celebrating all that God has done. Like a city too busy and crowded to receive the baby King, our hearts can suffer from long-term exposure.

After a dark, cold winter, our hearts can respond as if frostbitten. Enduring long hardships can cause us to put up walls to keep the hurt out. Will we ever feel joy and relief after this deep freeze? We certainly will; eventually, the precious signs of Spring start to show through. There is a scene in C. S. Lewis' *Chronicles of Narnia: The Lion, the Witch and the Wardrobe* that illustrates this beautifully. Aslan the lion is just about to offer his life as a sacrifice for Edmund's betrayal, and the White Queen's power has started to crack. Her hold on the land of "everlasting winter" has started to dissipate. The sight of running water and the dripping of melting ice off the trees brings excitement to the children and the creatures of the land. The White Queen's dreaded sleigh is no longer of use to her, and she is forced to walk, rendering her almost powerless. (Lewis, 1950)

It's like that in our spiritual battles. God delivers the victory over our foes, and we begin to see the signs of Spring. It is fresh and full of budding newness. Even when the change of seasons is for the better, we can be caught off guard. To better weather the changing season, we must realign as a team.

And the Cycle Begins Again—Springing Forward

In nature, spring follows winter. Often, we experience a quick turn in the weather. Sometimes we live with the chance of frost for a while. Rest assured, however, that the season of bitterness brings about growth and beauty if we give it the respect it deserves.

Making the Honeymoon Last—It's Not Over

Throughout this book, we have attempted to share how God has been faithful in every season. Like us, you may want to revisit seasons that are timely and sticking points in your marriage. We are also planning an expansion of each season, so keep your eyes out if that would help you.

- **Spring**: Changes can cause us to feel as if we are on shifting sand, but we can remain steady in our agreement building our marriages on the Rock.

- **Summer**: The "busyness" of our current culture can cause us to neglect what is truly important in our relationships with God and our spouse. By learning to calendar our important events, we can rest assured we are investing in our future.

- **Autumn**: This is a sweet time of slowing down, but it can be tempting to see it as being put out to pasture, as if our usefulness has run out. Quite the opposite is true. God is just getting started. He needs us to remain in the fight, working within our marriage mission.

- **Winter**: Though we experience cold, bitter trials around us, we can remain in unison, fighting together against our true enemy, the devil.

We are living proof that, if you are open to it, God has a great plan and provision to get you there. He has given you everything you need to continue growing, loving, and looking like Jesus. You are never finished until Jesus perfects you face-to-face. With a heart for God and your spouse, you cannot help but have a life full and abundant and rich! You will find yourself living the Honeymoon Life.

Happy Honeymooning!

ACKNOWLEDGMENTS

Jesus, unapologetically!

Next, because I needed them early on and still today: Lora Ross, Lisa Scala, Janet Herz, and Monique P. Taylor. These ladies have been with me in my developing years and have stuck by me no matter what.

Our family and friends in Iowa, especially Judi Johnson, Nana, you are forever a source of strength and joy. I needed a very large, loving support system all my life. God gave me you.

Jill Krupp, my "Jillustrator" and co-creative processor. All illustrations of birds in this book are available as prints. For more information, contact: Honeymoonlife808@gmail.com.

Curtis' amazing family and friends.

Pastor Robb and our amazing Grace Church Maui Ohana – too many to name! Aloha, Ke Akua! The Hula Ministry!

Lawn Doctor Franchisees and Franchisor; you made us so much better.

Our Texas friends and colleagues: CG Group, Polka Dots, numerous peer veteran business owners who push toward excellence, NACWE Rockwall, Pray and Serve group, and our loving community at Lake Pointe Church.

My amazing beta readers: Wes and Jennifer Oliver, Vernon and Joyce Goodman, Nathan and Audrey Hughes, Joan Allen, Shawn Talbot, Claudia Williams, Pastor Robb Finberg, and Curtis Krupp.

Bonnie Daneker of the Author's Greenhouse, without whom I would not have brought this message to a sensible conclusion.

Our amazingly supportive and loving children: Ariella Upton, Victoria Krupp, Alexander Krupp (Alex is also my website and social media assistant, designer, and technology help), and Phoebe "Max" Krupp, and our grandchildren Rion, Rory, Rowan, and Kai. I am so rich!

Curtis (crying as I write this), you have shown me the love of Jesus purer and richer than any woman can deserve. Your leadership, faith, and boldness within our family has been the second-best blessing in my life. Your unwavering devotion, support, and belief in me is well... crazy. To call you my best friend only scratches the surface.

NOTES

1   Digital Bible, 2023. "Understanding Birds In The Biblical Context: A Deep Dive Into Their Symbolism & Significance," *Digital Bible*. https://digitalbible.ca/article-page/bible-study-symbols-understanding-birds-in-the-biblical-context-a-deep-dive-into-their-symbolism-&-significance-1700845099124x347942094921580100

2   "Eastern Bluebird." Audubon, accessed December 8, 2024. https://www.audubon.org/field-guide/bird/eastern-bluebird.

3   "Newton's Laws of Motion." NASA, accessed June 27, 2024. https://www1.grc.nasa.gov/beginners-guide-to-aeronautics/newtons-laws-of-motion

4   Serra, Jack. 2001. *Marketplace, Marriage & Revival: The Spiritual Connection*. Orlando, FL: Longwood Communications.

5   Miller, Gia, Stephanie A. Lee, and Jodi Musoff. "The Benefits of Boredom." Child Mind Institute. Accessed November 13, 2024. https://childmind.org/article/the-benefits-of-boredom.

6   United States Secret Service. "Counterfeit Investigations." Accessed 2024. https://www.secretservice.gov/investigations/counterfeit.

7   "Balancing Marriage and Parenting." Marriage Dynamics Institute. Accessed May 7, 2019. https://marriagedynamics.com/keeping-love-alive-marriage-parenting

8   "'If You Want to Be Happy for the Rest of Your Life'—Study Finds Women of Faith Most Satisfied in Marriage." Catholic News Agency, May 22, 2019. https://www.catholicnewsagency.com/news/41343/if-you-want-to-be-happy-for-the-rest-of-your-life-study-finds-women-of-faith-most-satisfied-in-marriage.

9   Donald, Esther. "What Causes Gray Divorce? Reasons Why Older Couples Split." Goranson Bain Ausley, accessed March 3, 2025. https://gbfamilylaw.com/blogs/what-causes-gray-divorce-later-in-life-reasons-why-older-couples-split.

10 Carmody, Dennis P., and Michael Lewis. "Brain Activation When Hearing One's Own and Others' Names." National Library of Medicine, October 20, 2006. https://pmc.ncbi.nlm.nih.gov/articles/PMC1647299.

11 Maloney, Bree. "The Effects of Negativity." Marque Medical, November 8, 2022. https://marquemedical.com/effects-of-negativity.

RESOURCES

Scripture: Passages quoted from the Bible directly were taken from BibleGateway.com (NASB).

New American Standard Bible®(NASB), ©1960, 1971, 1977, 1995, 2020 by The Lockman Foundation. La Habra, CA. All rights reserved.

Spring

"Seeing Equinoxes and Solstices from Space." NASA. Accessed April 4, 2025. https://earthobservatory.nasa.gov/images/52248/seeing-equinoxes-and-solstices-from-space.

Boeckmann, Catherine. "Easter and the Paschal Full Moon." Almanac.com, accessed April 4, 2025. https://www.almanac.com/easter-paschal-full-moon.

Chapman, Gary D. *The Five Love Languages: A Journal*. Chicago Ill.: Northfield Pub, 2005.

Love Language Brand. "The Love Language® Quiz." Accessed in 2024. https://5lovelanguages.com/quizzes/love-language.

"Youversion Bible App." YouVersion, November 6, 2023. https://www.youversion.com/the-bible-app.

Niebuhr, Reinhold. *The Serenity Prayer*, 1932.

Gordon, Jon, and Damon West. *The Coffee Bean*. Hoboken, NJ: John Wiley and Sons, 2019.

Summer

LC. "Jesus' 7 Miracles He Performed on the Sabbath." Teachings of the Bible, September 14, 2016. https://teachingsofthebible.wordpress.com/2016/09/14/jesus-7-miracles-he-performed-on-the-sabbath/.

Muth, Natalie. "Benefits of Family Meals: Eat Together, Thrive Together." HealthyChildren.org, May 14, 2024. https://www.healthychildren.org/English/family-life/family-dynamics/Pages/family-meals-eat-together-thrive-together.aspx.

Helpful Reads

Barnhill, Julie A. *She's Gonna Blow! Real Help for Moms Dealing with Anger.* Harvest House Publishers, March 1, 2005.

Daneker, Bonnie B. *Stoplights are for Kissing: Easy Ways to Keep Love in Your Relationship.* The Author's Greenhouse, 2024.

Homan, Vincent D. *Foot in Two worlds: A Pastor's Journey from Grief to Hope.* Westbow Press, 2013.

About the Author

Terri "Harvester" Krupp

Growing up in rural Iowa, Terri wanted to be an astronaut. So, upon graduation she joined the Air Force, where she met the love of her life, Curtis.

They assumed that leaving the military would lead to a "normal" married life, but Curtis is a defense contractor, so they moved many times. Four children and four grandchildren later, Terri and Curtis remain best friends.

To satisfy her adventurous spirit, Terri has had many professional seasons: jailor, housewife, roads engineer, math/physics teacher, Tae Kwon Do studio manager (she holds a Black Belt), and franchise owner/operator. Currently, she is making herself available to Christian women as a mentor and coach.

Her greatest accomplishment is her lifelong love affair with Jesus.

Life Verse: "Pure and undefiled religion in the sight of our God and Father is this: to visit orphans and widows in their distress and to keep oneself unstained by the world." (James 1:27)

Contact Terri for speaking, seminars, and workshops at
honeymoonlife808@gmail.com

Check out all of our resources at
https://LivingtheHoneymoonLife.com

About the Illustrator

Jill Krupp

Jill is a third-generation Colorado native. She has always been creative. As a child, she made a cardboard record player with individual cardboard records (with their own sleeves!) for her Barbies. The player even had a paperclip bent to form a holder and arm for the records to spin.

Jill went to school for landscape design and took classes to become a master gardener. Jill married her high school sweetheart after college and went on to have three children.

Jill is always trying new creative projects, including needlework, sewing, card making, scrapbooking, and tole painting. She works in watercolors, colored pencils, acrylic markers, and combinations of the above. She has begun showing and selling her art, which includes colored pencil pet portraits and her new "Quilted Art Style."

Contact her for her bird artwork at:
honeymoonlife808@gmail.com

www.ingramcontent.com/pod-product-compliance
Lightning Source LLC
Chambersburg PA
CBHW041534120626
46551CB00019B/2692